"They used to say, 'If we find a good black player, we'll sign him.' They was lying."

Cool Papa Bell

TABLE OF CONTENTS

INTRODUCTION

Baseball is life. At least that's what I grew up thinking. Baseball was everything to me and it continues to be a major part of who I am as a middle-aged man. For much of America, this idealized version of baseball has permeated throughout society and suburban culture, but baseball is more than just a sport or a game, it's a microcosm of our country, especially with politics, culture, and race. Some people may see baseball as nothing more than a kid's game that some overpaid grownups get to play for a living, but the sport has long been a barometer of the nation's culture as a whole. In this book we explore the history of baseball and stories of exclusionary practices in the sport at every level relating to gender, race, sexual orientation, and other identities. Some of these stories relate to extremely famous ballplayers, like Vida Blue or Hank Aaron, but others are about the true unknowns whose careers were derailed or otherwise impacted by these very practices. Through these stories and experiences, we can gain a better understanding of why the game looks as it does today at all levels. This book is not meant to be an exposé on anyone specific nor is it designed to disparage the efforts of Major League Baseball in fighting these issues. In fact, one of the interviews is with Billy Bean, a high-ranking MLB official who specializes in Social Responsibility & Inclusion. This book is more about understanding the issue—to expose how pervasive these problems are throughout all levels of the game and to spark the necessary conversation to solve them. The many people who have helped in the creation of this book all had unique experiences, despite all facing a very similar villain. Everyone's experience with prejudice, bigotry, or hate is different and this book reflects that.

THE STORY OF WILMER AARON

Henry (Hank) Aaron was one of the greatest players in Major League Baseball (MLB) history. Born to a poor family in Mobile, Alabama, with seven siblings, he overcame the odds and became a Hall-of-Fame player. He hit 755 home runs (a record for many years before being broken by Barry Bonds), drove in 2,297 runs (still a record as of 2020), won a World Series, an MVP, several Gold Gloves, and batting titles, and was named an all-star 25 times. He is one of the most decorated players in history. But Hammerin' Hank, despite being a hero to so many, faced racism throughout his career. He began his professional career as a member of the Indianapolis Clowns of the Negro American League in late 1951, after Jackie Robinson had broken baseball's color barrier but before the end of mostly segregated baseball leagues, and was immediately confronted with overt racism right in Washington, D.C. "We had breakfast while we were waiting for the rain to stop, and I can still envision sitting with the Clowns in a restaurant behind Griffith Stadium and hearing them break all the plates in the kitchen after we finished eating. What a horrible sound. Even as a kid, the irony of it hit me: here we were in the capital in the land of freedom and equality, and they had to destroy the plates that had touched the forks that had been in the mouths of Black men. If dogs had eaten off those plates, they'd have washed them[i]."

As a minor leaguer, Aaron thrived. He quickly developed into a top prospect and was one of the best hitters in Minor League Baseball. Despite this, Aaron faced constant racism that nearly caused him to quit the game altogether, but his brother Herbert Jr. told him not to give up his opportunity[ii]. His next season, he was even better. He was so good that one sportswriter commented, "Henry Aaron led the league in everything except hotel accommodations[iii]." Because he was one of the few Black players at the time, Aaron encountered many challenges. He was required to stay in different hotels, to eat in different restaurants, and he often faced personal danger throughout the racially divided South under Jim Crow. As Aaron approached the then-

MLB Record of 714 home runs hit by the beloved Babe Ruth (who, notably also faced racism in the 1920s due to his appearance as a person who may have been of mixed heritage), he began to receive hate mail and death threats. He completed the 1973 season with 713 home runs and said that his only fear was that he might not live to see the 1974 season[iv]. The U.S. Post Office stated that he had received over 900,000 pieces of mail in 1973, and while most of the mail was supportive of Aaron, there was still a substantial amount of mail that was hateful or downright threatening. Aaron's chase of the record showed much of America that racism in baseball did not retire when Jackie Robinson entered the majors in 1947.

His brother Tommie enjoyed some minor success as well, but they were not the only members of the Aaron family trying to make it to the Majors. A cousin of theirs, Wilmer, has a very different story. Wil has enjoyed a successful career as a baseball coach and achieved more as a player than most, but for him the experience was less than ideal. He was a first-round pick in the

January 1971 draft and immediately enjoyed success at the minor league level, hitting .315 with a .408 OBP at Bluefield in Rookie level ball and ended up hitting close to .300 for his entire six-year minor league career. Unfortunately, he never made it past AA ball, partially because of his lack of power (he only hit 9 home runs in 2283 at bats in the minor leagues), but a lot had to do with the fact that he was converted into an outfielder despite being an excellent infielder.

Why would Baltimore try to convert Aaron? One reason might have been the presence of Rob Andrews, a future Major League second baseman (and coach of baseball camps I attended as a kid), but according to Wil, it was a lot more nefarious than that. When talking with Wil about his experience, he told me about how they took the Black players in camp and put them in center field because "that is where they belong". They took a look at him and said "he looks like an outfielder" despite being a truly prototypical second baseman at 5'8" and 155 pounds and possessing a skill and physical tool set that simply would not lead to the Major Leagues as an outfielder. Throughout his time in the minors he was bounced back and forth between the outfield and second and struggled to truly find his place. After a couple of years he joined the Indians organization and finally got to play second base on a consistent basis and was clearly the superior defensive second baseman on his team at the AA level. In 1976 he struggled defensively as he was moved back to a role where he played both second base and outfield. Nevertheless, his hitting certainly did not suffer, because he hit .308 (nobody else on the team hit over .286), leading the team in total bases, stolen bases (34, next most was 13), doubles, triples, hits, and runs scored. He also got hit by more pitches than anyone else on the team. Four non-pitching teammates from that team played in the Majors—Wil outhit them all.

Wil being coerced into switching positions was not an anomaly for sports as Black players in all sports have often been barred from certain positions. For many years, it was nearly impossible for a Black quarterback to reach the upper levels of the sport, and those who did often had to take circuitous routes to get there. Warren Moon had to dominate Canadian football for half a decade before the NFL gave him a chance. Several years before Moon's path to the NFL, Chuck Ealey challenged the conventions and potential position change by saying he would only play in the NFL if he could remain a quarterback, a position he was good enough at to place eighth in Heisman Trophy voting and be named to the All-American team. Ealey went undrafted and ended up starring in the Canadian Football League. The NFL never came calling. In English Premier League football (soccer to Americans), Black players not only experience racism, but they too find that certain positions are mostly off-limits to them. Out of Australia there is a blogger called "The Secret Footballer" and they claim that Premier League managers pigeonhole players into specific positions on the field based on their ethnicity. "Managers in the modern game just do not trust Black players in certain roles," they write, "and the tempo-controlling midfielder, the most important position in the game relative to how the team plays, is the role in which Black players are trusted the least."[v] And the stats seem to prove that: Despite being 35% Black as a league, only 10% of that extremely important position is made up of Black players. While 2020 may have been "the year of the Black quarterback," only time will tell if it is an anomaly or a new normal for the NFL in terms of Black players under center.

Changing positions was the norm for a lot of Black players throughout the post-integration period. There are no statistics on position changes, but there are statistics on the rate of Black players by position, and they show a dramatic positional bias by the various MLB franchises. Black players play outfield. There is no other way to put it. The franchises saw a player with dark skin and immediately said, "He belongs in the outfield". Few catchers in MLB history have been Black, and since 2005, when (the great) Charles Johnson retired, the league went several years before another Black catcher played a game. In the 2019 season, there was not a single Black starting catcher in the Major

Leagues[vi]. And anyone who has coached Little League can attest that seeing a Black kid behind the plate is extremely rare. In fact, in my entire coaching career (in both high school and Little League) I have only seen two Black catchers and I was the one who taught both to play the position. One such kid was such a phenomenal athlete behind the plate that my assistant coach and I joked even a decade later "E-Man would've had that" any time someone didn't get to a foul pop-up because...well, E-Man would've gotten it. Wil Aaron suffered his position change for the very same reason why E-Man was stuck as a backup outfielder (because he was not a strong hitter) until he was 14 and on my team—namely, he was Black and "looked like an outfielder" to his White coaches. It really is that simple. Players do not choose their positions, their positions are given to them by their coaches through the years. Outfield at the lower levels is boring for many kids, too, so the Black kids who get relegated to outfield duties often get bored with the game because they are rarely involved in the action.

Positional demographics at the Major League level are very telling. In figures 1, 2 & 3, notice how the league divides up the players by race and how it has shifted over time. The dramatic drop in White outfielders when the league integrated was not replicated with any kind of similar drop in White pitchers. If you look on the mound in any Major League game these days, your chances of seeing a Black pitcher are extremely low. In 2016, there were just 14 Black pitchers out of 449 total Major League pitchers: seven starters and seven relievers. Looking at the position-by-position chart of the Major Leagues, notice how much racial bias plays into positioning. In 2016 there were only 13 Black infielders in the entire league. That's just 1.5% of all players in the Major Leagues[vii].

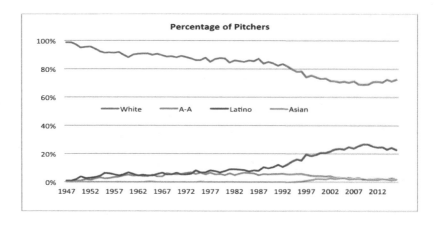

Figure 1

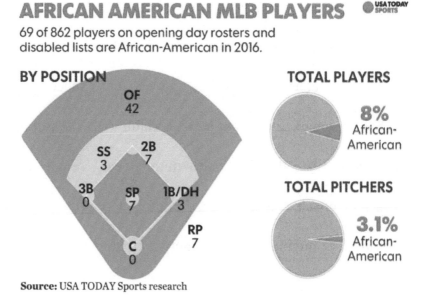

Figure 2

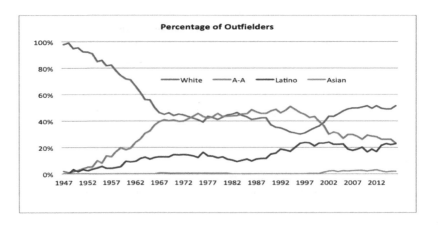

Figure 3

Positional bias was a major part of Wil's experience, but it goes deeper than that and the struggle has continued into his career as a coach. Aaron has enjoyed more success as a high school baseball coach than most, certainly more than I have, but his success has always come with a caveat. As any inner-city baseball coach can attest to, building a program without the community buying in is extremely difficult. For Wil, he faced these challenges as the coach at Serra High School in Los Angeles. "As you know, it is quite difficult putting a team together and being competitive when kids don't buy in. It is mandatory too for parents to be aboard. There just wasn't enough support and seriousness and coaching under these circumstance(s) became futile. It became less enjoyable and more stressful. It became far too much of a battle.[viii]" Coach Aaron was named the CIF "Coach of the Year," as well as being named "Coach of the Year" by the LA Times, The LA Sentinel, and The LA Wave Papers. He left Serra after the 2015 season because of the challenges of maintaining an elite program with so many obstacles.

He developed several MLB draft picks, including Dominic Smith, who was one of the National League's best hitters in 2020 [10th in batting average, second in doubles, fourth in OPS (on-base plus slugging percentage)], but even having an elite team like that one in 2013 did not help in recruiting a more consistent roster year-to-year. Smith was also a beneficiary of MLB's commitment to building up baseball in the inner-city: He was a part of the Urban Youth Academy team that won the RBI (Reviving Baseball in Inner Cities) Boys Junior Division Championship and even had a tryout for the national under-16 team as a result of his stellar play in that tournament. But Dominic Smith's path to MLB stardom was not without its challenges.

Smith's rise to the MLB did not distract him from his plight growing up in the inner city as a young Black man. "Silence kills" is the line that Dominic used when he so eloquently voiced his concern for the plight of Black people in the United States. When George Floyd, Breonna Taylor, and several others suffered the same deadly fate at the hands of police, Smith did not remain silent like many of his peers among the MLB elite. Instead, he took to social media on Twitter and provided his fans with his perspective.

"As a Black man in America, you encounter racism on every level. Your parents prep you for it. They prep you for routine police stops. They prep you on how to talk to people with respect. When you have one strike against you (your skin color), you have to make the people

you come across like you, and you do it with respect, with a smile, with love. I didn't understand it as a kid. I went to predominantly Black schools my whole life, so when I got into the real world, it hit me. I saw how we were oppressed firsthand. Whether it's education, job opportunities, healthcare, mass incarceration, social programs, financial hardship, and more. I saw how I wasn't equal and treated unfairly because of my skin color."

Smith also highlighted the names of several Black people who have been the victims of police violence, including George Floyd, Ahmaud Arbery, and Breonna Taylor. He added that it's a duty for people to speak up when they witness injustice. *"The system has been killing African-Americans and minorities for hundreds of years, and enough is enough!*

I don't want to fear being stopped by a police officer or looked down (on) because of my skin color! It shouldn't have taken the death of so many innocent men and women for the world to take notice. And if we didn't have social media or smartphones, how many more innocent lives would we have lost? **Silence kills[ix].** "

Smith's role as one of the most prominent Black stars in the MLB means his voice was heard. But who actually got that message? Even his so-called fans had objections to his message. One such "fan" stated, "You had me until you mentioned BLM (Black Lives Matter). Then I realize (sic) you weren't for change, but just wanted more Democrats to get elected." Generally, retweets of random people on the internet are a waste of words, but this one seemed pertinent to the situation because of what it represents. It was a minority of the responses to his powerful tweet, but what it showed is that there are still many out there who see a Black player and think "just hit the damn ball, I don't care what you think." This mentality is especially pervasive in the fandom of Major League Baseball partially, because MLB fans are 60% White and just 16% Black[x]. With the political makeup of baseball fans being 32% Republican and 30% Independent, Smith risked alienating more than half the fan base by coming out with that statement. This is partially why baseball has been slow to adjust to the changing mentality of America when it comes to race relations. The NBA and NFL have far more outspoken activists (in the NBA there are even several White coaches who have been extremely vocal on the Black Lives Matter movement, such as Steve Kerr and Gregg Popovich) than Major League Baseball and that could possibly be attributed to the fan demographics.

Back in 2013, when the Serra team was on its way to the CIF title, the defending MLB champion San Francisco Giants had no Black players. Neither did the St Louis Cardinals. But the Serra team was on its way to be the first predominantly Black team to win a Southern Section baseball championship. As one of the players stated in an interview with the LA Times, "In the inner-city, all you hear is that baseball is racist", and that can really go a long way in perpetuating the idea that baseball is not a sport for Black players. During the season, people were seeing Serra as a beacon of hope for inner-city baseball: "Everyone is hoping that Serra's success stirs the area, stirs the neighborhood, and makes great young athletes say, 'Hey, maybe we want to play that sport,'" said longtime Arizona area scout Hal Kurtzman[xi]. Unfortunately, this spectacular season was a flash-in-the-pan and Aaron was gone from the program just 30 months later. He had turned around a 1-26 program into a nationally known one, but realized quickly that there were factors at play that would keep him from building a truly lasting program in the inner-city. He used a "get on board or get left" mentality to build the program despite a lot of reluctance from the school, administrators, and even the players.

Coaching high school baseball comes with a lot of

challenges (more on this later), but for Wilmer those challenges were enough to drive him away soon after guiding his team to the CIF title. Without a steady stream of travel ball players coming in, it is extremely difficult to maintain a successful tradition. Schools in affluent areas do not have the same problems, because there are dozens of travel ball players vying for a chance to be a part of those programs. Wilmer's program enjoyed a brief ride to the top before it crashed back down due to a weak pipeline of talent coming in. The year the Varsity team won the title and had a future MLB star on its roster, the Junior Varsity team went 0-8 and then followed that winless season with another one. The lack of a successful Junior Varsity team does not guarantee a program's failure at the Varsity level, but it certainly does not help a program sustain itself. Following the big 27-5 season, Serra went 13-13 and then 13-16 before Wil moved on from coaching at the Gardena high school.

Serra High School in Gardena may have the same name as the school where Barry Bonds went a few hundred miles up the 101, but the differences are otherwise quite significant. Serra High School in San Mateo, CA, is a famous baseball factory in an affluent suburb of San Francisco that has produced dozens of professional baseball players, including Barry Bonds, Gregg Jefferies, and 2019 first-round draft pick Hunter Bishop. It is an all-boys Catholic school, charges tuition, and most of the students come from wealthy, educated families. It also has an extremely White student population, with ~60% of the students being White. The number of Black students was just 11, or 1.1% of the 985 boys attending in 2019[xii].

The demographics at Serra High School in Gardena are very different. Instead of having just around one dozen Black students, Serra in Gardena had 13 White students, and 70% of the students are Black. These stark differences between the two like-named schools in California shows how different the situations are in different neighborhoods. Gardena is a relatively poor area, with more than 15% of the population falling below the poverty line,[xiii] while San Mateo's poverty rate was about one-third of that of Gardena's[xiv]. Racially, San Mateo and Gardena are also quite different, with San Mateo only being about 2% Black compared to Gardena being about 25% Black. Many other factors come into play for both of these schools and the strength of their baseball programs, but there's no denying the racial and economic differences between these two cities in California. Both schools are Catholic and private, but one caters almost exclusively to Black students, whereas the other serves mainly White and Asian students.

I met Wilmer through a mutual connection on LinkedIn. It was a random request out of the blue after I had engaged in a discussion about racism in baseball on someone's else's post. He said to me, "I love your message on LinkedIn! You seem like you understand the politics and racism going on. I'd like to fill you in....I played 6 years professionally and was one of the best. I was Blackballed out after refusing to sign my contract again with the Indians. I will explain to you exactly how they do it. This is all planned. I still have nightmares to this day of maltreatment[xv]." Wilmer goes on to share a deluge of stories and information about his experience and the experiences of some of his players, including several future Major Leaguers. Every couple of weeks over the next several months I received more emails with more examples of racial hostility in baseball. One such story involved Lyman Bostock.

Lyman Bostock was a great player in the mid/late 1970s. He played from 1975 to 1978 and had a career .311 batting average while also playing centerfield at an elite level. He even received votes for the MVP award in 1977 and 1978 and was said to be so good that (Hall-of-Fame manager) Earl Weaver predicted that he would "win five or six batting titles before his career is over". He was seen as a caring person who was destined to be a coach one day. But that was before the fateful night in Gary, Indiana[xvi]. Bostock was not even the target of the bullet that killed him. Bostock met Barbara Smith at a dinner party his uncle, Ed Turner, was hosting. Afterward, Smith, Bostock, Turner, and Smith's sister, Joan Hawkins, got into Turner's car and started driving to Hawkins' home. At some point, Leonard Smith, Barbara's estranged husband, drove up alongside Turner and began chasing him. Turner ran several red lights, but then hit congestion and was forced to stop. Smith got out of his car with a small-gauge shotgun, fired a single shot into the back seat of Turner's car, and hit Bostock, instead of Barbara, his intended victim. Actually, Barbara was hit by a single pellet in the neck, but Bostock took the rest of the shot in the right side of his head. He was taken to St. Mary's Medical Center and declared dead there about three hours later[xvii].

The tragic story of Bostock was not one that seems related to Aaron's on the surface, but the two men had a significant impact on each other. According to Wilmer, Lyman was slumping in 1978 when Aaron had a conversation with him. They had some hard words with each other, but those hard words seemed to impact Bostock significantly because he snapped out of the slump soon after. The loss of Bostock deeply affected Wilmer, not only for the loss of a friend but also for the loss of what Bostock could become after his playing days were over—namely, a coach or manager and an advocate for the game in the inner-city. Unfortunately for everyone, Bostock's life came to an end two months shy of his 28th birthday. The loss of Bostock may have robbed future generations of a strong Black role model, but the true tragedy of his loss is that his impact was never truly felt in the league as it should have been. Bostock was beloved by his peers and this excerpt from his eulogy sums it up so beautifully: "We called him Jibber Jabber because he enlivened every clubhouse scene, chasing tension, drawing laughter in the darkest hour of defeat. When winning wasn't in the plan, Lyman knew the sun would come up the next morning…. There's only one consolation: We're all better persons for having him touch our lives[xviii]."

The impact of Bostock's death was significant on Wil and he is still affected by it more than 40 years later. However, Bostock and Aaron had very different paths in baseball. Bostock reached the Majors after being relatively fast-tracked through the system, spending one year in each minor league level and being promoted to the MLB at age 24. He was a great hitter and a natural outfielder. He did not suffer the fate of Aaron being shifted around from position to position while trying to develop into a Major League Baseball player. The 1978 season was eventful for Bostock beyond the way it tragically ended. On April 30, following an 0-for-4 effort against Toronto that dropped his average to .147, Bostock told the media that, having been rebuffed by Gene Autry (owner of the California Angels) in his attempt to refuse that month's paycheck, he would give his April salary to charity. "I just can't make that kind of money and not produce," he said. "I don't feel that I've done enough for this month.[xix]" The type of integrity it took for a man to forego his salary because he did not believe he was performing well enough to deserve it just shows us the kind of man the world lost when that bullet hit him in Gary, Indiana. Bostock's family never really got any resolution either, because his killer worked the legal system and barely served any time as a result. I tell the story of Lyman Bostock not only because it is a tragic story of loss in the game of baseball, but also because of what Bostock represented.

He was part of a generation of Black ballplayers who were taking the game by storm. Kids who grew up in the 1970s and 1980s grew up watching a game where Black players made up more than 15% of the league, but that number is less than 7% now and falling fast. You might think that the drop of Black participation in the MLB is related to the increase in Latin and Asian players, but when the decline in Black players began in the 1990s, the number of White players was not impacted at all. White participation was at 63.2% in 1996 and Black participation was at 16.0%, in 2016 Whites made up 63.7% of the league and Blacks were at 6.7%. In the attached chart, you can see the drastic shift in the league's racial makeup over time.

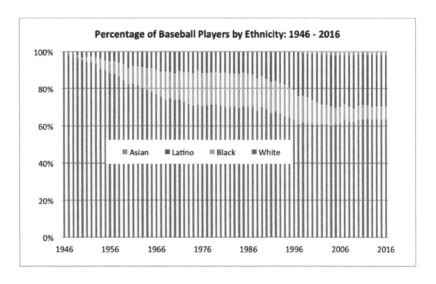

Percentage of Baseball Players by Ethnicity: 1946 - 2016

Figure 4[xx].

The loss of Lyman Bostock does not really factor into this timeline directly, but his loss was significant nevertheless. Every single Black role model in baseball played a major role in keeping the sport alive in the Black community, so the loss of someone as compelling as Bostock would be felt by many. The number of kids who could have been inspired by a string of Bostock batting titles and charity events will never be known.

Wil's career was not devoid of good people: He mentioned guys like Larry Anderson, Ed Arsenault, Dennis Eckersley, and Glenn Redmon as some of his allies during his time in the minors. The story he told about Redmon makes Redmon look like a truly selfless hero. Redmon was an excellent second baseman and had been given a brief stint in the Major Leagues before being sent back down to AA as a 28-year-old. He must have seen that his career was coming to an end, but that does not change the fact that Wil's experience was deeply impacted by Redmon's final days as a professional baseball player. While working out at second base with Redmon before a game one day, Glenn asked Wil why he was not playing second base, and Wil began to explain the situation with his unwanted position changes and his general plight as a minor leaguer. Glenn felt bad and said that he knew Wil deserved to play there. The very next day, Glenn packed up his gear and left the team to give Wil a better shot at getting time at second base. Redmon spent the next 40 years working as a teacher and coach and impacted thousands of other ballplayers in his second career.

While Wilmer Aaron does not appear in the annals of baseball history the way his relative Henry does, for Wil, the issues with what happened with him go beyond simply playing the game of baseball. Wil truly sees the issue creating deeper problems within the community. "The danger in this treatment is that Black players begin to believe they are 'inferior!' Some end up with mental illness problems! One of my friends that I played high school baseball against was with the Orioles, after they moved him from second base to the outfield he was found in his hotel room banging his bat in his hands over and over as if he was in a trance. They will start drinking, doing drugs or just walk around with guilt like they weren't good enough. It is tragic the number of Afro-American kids who are ruined by racism![xxi]"

Aaron is clearly living with a lot of "what if" to this day when he reflects on his time as a player. His experience shaped his future and how he's approached the game as a coach and ambassador for the sport. His story needed to be told because these kinds of stories generally are lost in the anonymity of the person telling it. By putting Wil's story out there, I hope to inspire others who went through the same process to put theirs out there, too. One can only imagine the number of players who were told to leave their best position in favor of the crowded group in the outfield. How many young catchers were told to play center field simply because of the color of their skin? It is hard enough to make it as a ballplayer, even when you have everything going your way, so being told to change positions becomes another major obstacle.

CURT FLOOD

When people talk about the greatest center fielders in the history of baseball, the usual suspects tend to come up: Ken Griffey Jr., Willie Mays, Mike Trout, Mickey Mantle, Ty Cobb, and Joe DiMaggio. Cool Papa Bell and Oscar Charleston factor into those discussions, too, if the people debating are true scholars of the game, but as "what if?" subjects rather than truly being in the debate. But there are some others who often creep into the conversation, too, because of their defensive prowess despite some offensive flaws or other factors that keep people from grouping them with the all-time greats. Guys like Jim Edmonds, Carlos Beltran, Kirby Puckett, Richie Ashburn, Tris Speaker, and Andruw Jones also factor into a lot of people's rankings for the position's all-time best, however none of these players had the impact on ALL professional sports as much as Curt Flood. Oddly enough, like Wilmer Aaron, Flood was converted to the outfield from his more natural spot in the infield at third base. Flood accepted *that* move, but it was a move later in his career that he would *not* accept that cemented his place in sports history.

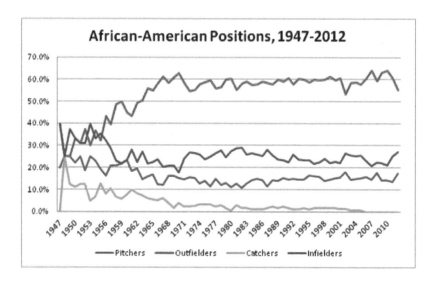

Figure 5[xxii]

Baseball is a game where the positions have a certain hierarchy at the lower levels. In Little League, there are countless kids who fill roles based on the stereotypes. In leagues where most of the kids are White, you will nearly always see the Black kid on the team playing Centerfield. For many coaches the choices on where to put players is based on a standardized template, where each position has an archetype, and unfortunately for many minority kids that means they will be placed somewhere based on what they look like rather than how they play. Figure 5 shows us the way Black players were able to reach the MLB based on their primary positions. The pattern is clear: The opportunities for Black players were nearly exclusive to the outfield. There were Black players at every position throughout the post-integration era, but as time moved forward those opportunities at other positions began to shrink with several years actually having no Black MLB catchers. Outfield makes up 33% of MLB positions, yet 60% of Black players who made the MLB since the mid-1960s have been outfielders. Like Wilmer Aaron, Flood was told that his best path to the Majors was in the outfield, but unlike Aaron, Flood did not fight the position shift. One has to wonder how many great Black outfielders in the Majors were actually on their way to being great shortstops, catchers, or third basemen. Moreover, how many other stories just like Wilmer Aaron's are out there?

Curt Flood was a great player. He made the All-Star team

three times and won seven consecutive Gold Gloves while being a very strong hitter for the St. Louis Cardinals, one of the best teams in baseball at the time. He covered tons of ground, recording more outs than any other outfielder in the National League during the late 1960s, and he had a strong arm, too. But Flood's story is about more than just his performance on the field—it is about his battle for players' rights, which cemented his place in history and arguably makes him a worthy Hall-of-Fame candidate, despite not achieving certain statistical benchmarks. Flood was a player whose importance goes well beyond the short window of time he had to display his athletic talents. He's a player who will be remembered a hundred years or more after his retirement and that seems to me to be a pretty darned good reason to enshrine him in Cooperstown.

Flood died back in 1997, so a conversation with him was out of the question, but I was able to get in touch with his son. Greatness is often seen in how those closest to a person remember them, and with Curt Flood, Jr. (to be referred to as

"Junior" from here on out), it was obvious the impact his father had on him. Junior has spent many years working hard to cement his father's legacy and has been involved in the push to have him enshrined as a player in Cooperstown. In speaking with Junior, the perspective I was given on Flood the man was of a loving and doting father who cared deeply for those closest to him and who felt immense pain from the racism and hate thrown his way. Throughout the conversation, Junior frequently lamented his father's lack of recognition as a player and how his fight for rights often overshadowed the great player he truly was. Flood's book, *A Well-Paid Slave*, provides enormous insight into Flood's experience fighting to establish free agency in MLB (and by extension into all other major professional sports). Thankfully Flood was able to get his thoughts and feelings down on paper for us to experience what he went through.

After the 1969 season, the St. Louis Cardinals traded their star center fielder, Curt Flood, to the Philadelphia Phillies, setting off a chain of events that would change professional sports forever. At the time there were no free agents and players did not have no-trade clauses. When a player was traded, he had to report to his new team or retire. Unwilling to leave St. Louis and influenced by the civil rights movement, Flood chose to sue Major League Baseball for his freedom. His case reached the Supreme Court, where Flood ultimately lost. But by challenging the system, he created an atmosphere in which, just three years later, free agency became a reality. Flood's decision ultimately cost him his career, but it made him a hero with a legacy that goes well beyond his amazing ability to track down a fly ball and to move Lou Brock from second to third with a well-placed ground ball.

For Flood, the story of his rise to the Majors was about overcoming the challenges of the Civil Rights movement but doing so very quickly and at a very young age. Flood was just 20 when he became an MLB regular, so he did not spend much time playing in small towns in the deep South like many of his peers, but he still spent a couple years playing in North Carolina and Georgia and had to face some serious headwinds. He started with the Reds organization, but it became clear that it would not be a permanent thing. "Vada Pinson, Frank Robinson, and Curt all came out at the same time for $4,000 apiece. The unspoken law at the time was that if you ever saw three guys on the team who were Black, one of them was about to be traded. That's what happened with my dad; he was shipped to St. Louis.[xxiii]" Flood dominated Minor League pitching and made it difficult for the Cardinals to keep him down there long. Flood was excelling despite having to get dressed in a separate clubhouse, sleeping and eating in separate facilities, and often being heckled by drunk, racist fans.

Many players experience a bad coach at some point in their lives, but it becomes something far worse when that coach is directly impacting your livelihood. It is one thing to have a jerk coaching you in Little League, but in the Major Leagues before free agency, that coach has you trapped. For Curt Flood, it was Solly Hemus, his second manager as a full-time Major

Leaguer. Hemus was known for having told Bob Gibson that he should give up on baseball (the same Bob Gibson who became a Hall-of-Famer) and he made life for Flood miserable. Hemus often used racial slurs around his Black players and Flood's performance suffered. In 1961, Hemus' last with the team, the negative impact of his presence was reflected in the performance of the Cardinals. The Cardinals were 33-41 when Hemus was fired, then went 47-33 the rest of the season. But nobody was more impacted by the departure of Hemus than Flood. He went from being a bench player batting in the .280s to a key piece of the lineup batting .322. He had a weight lifted from him when Hemus was gone and was an All-Star within a couple years.

Flood's journey could have ended with him simply being an excellent baseball player with an outside shot at the Hall-of-Fame if he continued hitting .300 for several more years to get near the magic 3,000-hit barrier (he had 1,854 at age 31 when the Cardinals tried to sell him), but Flood had other ideas. He was no longer going to sit back and let other people decide his future—he was going to take charge. Flood knew the potential sacrifices of fighting back and by doing so, he set in motion a movement that has caused professional athletes to rise from mere pawns to serious power brokers. Players today have immense power, and much of that is owed to Flood's sacrifices. Unfortunately for Flood, much of his impact was felt only by the next generation of athletes and not by himself.

After his Supreme Court case failed, Flood's mission did not end and the MLB Players Union was able to eventually strike down the reserve clause in 1975. In 1976, free agency began in Major League Baseball, setting in motion a process which sent salaries skyrocketing. In 1976, the highest paid player in the Major Leagues was Hank Aaron at $240,000. In 1990, the highest paid player was Robin Yount at $3,200,000. By 2019 that top salary, earned by pitcher Stephen Strasburg, was up to $38,333,333. The average salary has gone from $51,501 in 1976[xxiv] to ~$4,170,000 in 2021[xxv]. One of the beneficiaries of these changes was Alex Rodriguez, who earned more than

$445,000,000 in salary during his career[xxvi] and has built a business empire largely thanks to the sacrifices made by Flood in the early 1970s. In 2021, the San Diego Padres paid their four starting infielders a total of $66,000,000[xxvii] and had committed to long-term contracts worth over $800,000,000 to those four men. Unfortunately for Flood and his family, he never saw that kind of wealth, and his story took a dark turn after his fight with MLB.

His failure to win his case led Flood to a European exile, fleeing to Majorca, Spain, to become a bar owner. While there he began to truly deal with bouts of depression, loneliness, and alcohol dependency. Eventually, he was beaten up by the Spanish police and hospitalized with a fractured arm as a result of the beating. That point seemed to be his rock bottom and he eventually returned home to Oakland, as a broken man[xxviii]. Flood bounced back and began a full psychological healing and restoration process to return to health and happiness. He was welcomed by the MLB Players Union with open arms and at the national meeting in Atlanta in 1996 he was honored with a standing ovation. Unfortunately, Curt died in 1997 (he was only 59 years old), succumbing to throat cancer and leaving a hole in the world where the gravity of his impact was felt by many.

When speaking to Junior about the current landscape of baseball in the inner-city, he spoke frankly about the shift that has happened over the past few decades. "First and foremost, it's an economic thing. For every superstar Black kid they can find, it's just as easy to find dozens of Dominican kids. It's easier to put a basketball hoop up than it is to assemble the real estate, equipment, and nine other guys to play baseball. Plus, the NBA has done a remarkable job in marketing their product to the youth of America, especially Black kids." It is hard to argue with any of his points, and it becomes even more clear that the issue baseball is facing in the inner-city is a problem where the solution is unlikely to be one that can just be attained by throwing piles of cash at it. Junior had a father that he revered, the athletic talent to play baseball, and the pedigree to get noticed by scouts (being a Jr. helps a LOT when Sr. was an All-Star), but he focused far more on football and socializing. "I was more motivated by football and did not have that motivation for baseball. Plus, I also enjoyed the attention girls gave the football players." I can speak from experience, in high school we had few girls (that weren't already dating one of us) at our baseball games, but the football games had bleachers full of them. "I really loved and enjoyed the game, but not enough to put in that extra effort to get to the next level."

The story of Curt Flood tells us that the strength of our impact is often unrelated to our personal experience. We can give so much of ourselves to the movements we dedicate our time to without actually benefiting from any of our actions. These sacrifices made by people like Flood often cut deep and take so much from those making the sacrifices, but as long as we celebrate their legacies, the struggles will not be in vain. Flood's life may not have been ideal, but his impact was significant enough that his legacy is carried on by his family. In the end, the goal of any person with a family should be to do something significant enough in their lifetime that their children have a legacy to carry on.

MY EXPERIENCE AS A PLAYER

I am White. Well, I'm actually from a Jewish background and that factors into my viewpoint as a ball player, coach, and fan. Growing up, I was obsessed with the sport. I liked all sports, but something about baseball just hooked me. It may have been the history and the stats, or the tall tales of the ballplayers of the olden days that drew me in, but playing the game truly connected with my spirit. I studied that history and focused on the players that I could relate to. Sandy Koufax and Hank Greenberg were the only major stars that were truly celebrated for being Jewish, so I naturally followed them, but I also gained a massive amount of respect for the Negro League players after reading about their exploits and an obsession formed in my soul.

My favorite of those players was a guy named Cool Papa Bell. Bell was so fast that there were legends like the one Satchel Paige famously shared: "One time he hit a line drive right past my ear. I turned around and saw the ball hit him sliding into second," or the one that said that he was so fast he could flip the light switch and be in bed before the room got dark. One of my other favorite players as a kid was Rickey Henderson and all the stories of Bell made me imagine a player even faster than him. Satchel Paige was another player with all kinds of amazing tall tales, so I idolized the great teams like the Birmingham Barons, Kansas City Monarchs, or Homestead Grays.

I studied their stats, read about them, and even wrote my junior year history thesis paper on them. I have a huge collection of Negro League items, books, and shirts. As a kid I often wore Negro League apparel, and when asked who my favorite old-time players were, guys like Paige, Bell, Josh Gibson, Oscar Charleston, Rube Foster, Buck Leonard, etc., would come before guys like Joe DiMaggio, Ted Williams, Hack Wilson, Rogers Hornsby and Al Kaline. To me, the stars of the Negro Leagues were just elite baseball players to be revered like any great MLB player. I could not understand why people would keep such exciting players separate and excluded from Major League

Baseball until I was older and could grasp the concepts of segregation and racism.

As a player, I spent hours in my backyard pretending to be a Major League player, creating scenarios and making up locations in the yard to represent the bases. I would hit the ball and then run the bases, pretending there was a fielder trying to throw me out. I would even keep score of these imaginary games. I would also announce the games, generally as an Al Michaels type, but sometimes I'd throw in a little Bob Uecker humor in there...another obsession of mine as a child was *Major League*, a movie I easily watched over 500 times in my lifetime. I'd pitch against the fence and call my game. "Pasternack throws a fastball on the outside corner, strike!", is what I'd say unless the pitch was wild, then I would give the "Juuuuuuust a bit outside" call made famous in that movie. I loved to hit, but the part of baseball I loved most was throwing the ball. I pitched and pitched and pitched. Every single day. I threw until my arm hurt, and eventually, I threw until I put a hole in the fence. My parents bought me a target to throw at when they had to pay to fix the hole I made.

Unfortunately, I struggled to find the strike zone until I was a junior in high school and only got to enjoy one full season before my arm began to break down. I had surgery on my shoulder the summer after my senior year, and when I got to college, I needed to heal quickly to become part of a top program. I came back way too soon, pitched in four games in the fall (just 5⅔ innings, though I did strike out 14 batters) and after pitching in a tournament championship winning game against Texas A&M's club team, I ordered tortilla soup during our celebratory dinner at "On the Border" and realized that I couldn't lift my arm above my chest. I turned to my teammates and said, "I'm done, guys. This is it for me." Thus, I gave up on my dreams of playing baseball at the next level. I played semi-pro for a year and men's league for a few years after I graduated from college and even went to Cuba and pitched a game against Cuban players (actually, my very last game pitched) retired from the Cuban National Series and numerous former members of the Cuban National Team. But I knew at that point that the pain up and down my arm was just too much and my body was simply not cut out for it. Despite the bittersweet end to my career, baseball was responsible for many of my fondest memories and I was determined to help a new generation live out similar ones.

My struggle in baseball never really intersected with my looks or my cultural background. My struggle was physical. First, it was a lack of skill and physical talent, then it was my body breaking down. I had financial means to play the game and receive incredible coaching from former major leaguers like Fred Breining, Terry Whitfield, and many others. I always had a good glove (well, a quality glove...I was actually a pretty terrible defensive player), a backup glove, and whichever bat I wanted. My cleats always fit (kinda, I have weird feet and I grew like 6 shoe sizes one school year) and I never had pants with holes in them for more than a week or two. Despite all that, I never felt like I belonged. Maybe it was because I didn't celebrate Christmas or Easter, went to the weird private school, or went to the temple every Sunday instead of church, but maybe it was because I literally saw the world differently than most of my peers.

I played my first several years of Little League in a league that was made up of kids from extremely wealthy and extremely White neighborhoods. Most of the other kids from my synagogue were not very athletic and the only other baseball player I knew of was one of my best friends, but he lived one city over so we never got to play in the same league. On my teams, I was usually the only kid who didn't go to church on Sunday and who thought Easter was only about candy. Sometimes there was an Asian kid on my team, but seeing a player who was Black or Latino was extremely rare. I usually gravitated towards those other kids who were outside the norm and, as a result, I have very few long standing friendships with teammates from my baseball playing career. On the surface, I would seem just like the rest of the kids, but there was always something that made me feel like an outsider in the place where I should have felt like I belonged the most.

I played American Legion ball in high school on one of the best teams in the country. We won a pretty big tournament with 40 teams from around the nation and if not for a few bad bounces and a TON of injuries, we probably could have competed for the national title in 2000. But on that team I was an outsider because I came from a prep school in New Hampshire and only lived in California during the summer. I did not have any preexisting relationships with the team other than growing up in the area and facing some of them on the field over the years. The team was mostly White, there were a few kids that were Latino, Asian, Samoan, etc., but I don't recall a single Black kid on the team. This was not rare in the Bay Area, where most teams had some kids with Hispanic names and there were a couple of random kids of Asian descent, but only a handful of Black kids in the region. I distinctly remember facing a few teams that had a couple of Black kids on them, but the overwhelming majority of standout ballplayers in the area at the time were White.

They did not exclude me—I was even introduced to a summer fling by one of them, but as soon as summer was over we would forget all about each other. My general nature is to observe people when I don't feel part of the group. On my team, I was mainly just the closer and occasional left-handed bat off the bench, so I would spend most of the game stretching, drinking Sobe Wisdom (my beverage of choice at the time), and cracking the occasional joke. During the tournament in 1999, we were in Mesa, Arizona. It was July 4th week and the team was celebrating winning the whole thing by ordering up a couple of strippers to our motel. I'm not too sure where our coaches were, but we got pretty hectic. Alcohol, random girls from Scottsdale that we met at a red light, and strippers with about 35 guys (we had two teams, the Reds and the Blues) aged 15–18 riding an adrenaline high. Only one other guy and I decided it was too much for us and we went to the hot tub with the sisters of a couple of our teammates and talked about how we didn't understand how the guys could be like that. That was when I truly realized how different I was. There was a groupthink mentality that I simply could not fathom. It wasn't the action taken by the guys that surprised me, it was the lack of any divergence in thought from any of them that did.

I also played soccer for about 10 years growing up. As far as I can remember, my teams were exclusively White/Asian. One year we made it to the area playoffs and faced a team from East Palo Alto, which was actually the national per-capita murder capital of the country at the time[xxix], and my teammates were terrified. I couldn't understand why until I saw the other team. None of the players were White and they were all quite large compared to us. My teammates were intimidated by the color of their skin (they talked a lot about their ethnicity during our pregame) and there was a lot of chippy play during the game. For many of my teammates, it was the first time they had ever been involved in a sport with kids from outside the posh Hillsborough area.

We lost, but at the end of the tournament I was awarded the sportsmanship award for the whole tournament. Maybe it was because I kept my cool in the face of brutal losses, but it was likely because I remained committed to playing the game hard and did not try to fight with any of the kids who physically bullied me on that field. Even today when I play rec league hockey, I am always intense but also constantly chatting up the other team and celebrating success not just for myself and my team, but also congratulating a goalie when he robs me of a goal or when a defender intercepts one of my passes.

At the time of that soccer tournament, I had no idea what it all meant, but looking back on the experience I am much more clear on what that game represented. It was the moment our forcefield collapsed. We no longer lived in our bubble of rich White kids. While most of those players remained within the bubble, I saw this world of diverse teams and wanted in. I went home that day and asked my parents to take me out of the Burlingame-Hillsborough Little League and Hillsborough AYSO, to sign me up for a basketball league at a rec center, and to put me into a more diverse baseball league (San Mateo PONY-Colt), so I could escape the bubble. It was eye-opening, but I was much more at home in my new world. I transferred to a public school from my private school and got to truly be exposed to the real world for the first time. I eventually went back to private school (Exeter), but that was mainly because of issues at home that I wanted to remove myself from. I also wanted to play ice hockey at a higher level and I felt that a New England prep school would offer me that opportunity.

Once at Exeter, I immediately made friends with a number of guys from the football team, but none of them were White despite Exeter being a mostly White school. I was an outsider there, being from California and being more of a jock than a typical student at the school. I was not comfortable around most of the kids there because they grew up in a world I did not understand. Privileged White kids from Upstate New York, Boston suburbs, and Connecticut were simply a different breed than me. I could not identify with them in any way, so I tended to only associate with other outsiders there. I had plenty of friends at Exeter, but they were all from different cliques or groups and most of them were either international or kids from the ABC (A Better Chance) program, where kids from low income areas are given full rides to attend a prep school. This perspective has informed my entire adult life.

FLEET WALKER

A lot of people think of Jackie Robinson when talking about the first Black players in the top tiers of professional baseball, but in reality the first Black man to play at that level was a catcher named Moses Fleetwood "Fleet" Walker back in 1884. To most baseball fans, Fleet Walker is mostly the answer to an obscure trivia question, as shown in the classic 1990s baseball movie *Little Big League*. In the movie, the main character (Billy Heywood) and his grandfather play baseball trivia games. The young Billy asks his grandfather who the first Black player in the Major Leagues was, and his grandfather's response is, "You want me to say 'Jackie Robinson', but I won't. Fleet Walker for Toledo, I believe the year was 1884." He even had a younger brother who also played baseball, but Fleet's legacy was that of the final man to play Major League Baseball before segregation. Walker has a place in history, but more as a Homer Plessy kind of historical figure rather than a Ruby Bridges or Jackie Robinson. He enjoyed some success at the

Major League level with the Toledo baseball club and appeared to have a bright future in the game until Cap Anson came to town.

Cap Anson was a big star and later a member of the Baseball Hall of Fame. He was also an extremely outspoken racist and bigot. His refusal to step on the field for a game while Walker was on it was the beginning of what became a de facto rule throughout the Major Leagues. This is the incident that created the so-called "color barrier". Walker's experience dealing with racism was significant even within his own teams. During his career he played with at least two fellow players who were open segregationists. One was outfielder Curt Welch, who played both the 1883 and 1884 seasons as Walker's teammate; the other was Tony Mullane, Toledo's workhorse pitcher in 1884. "He [Walker] was the best catcher I ever worked with, but I disliked a Negro and whenever I had to pitch to him I used to pitch anything I wanted without looking at his signals. One day he signaled me for a curve and I shot a fast ball at him. He caught it and came down to me....He said, 'I'll catch you without signals, but I won't catch you if you are going to cross me when I give you signals.' And all the rest of that season he caught me and caught anything I pitched without knowing what was coming."[xxx] Anyone who has ever caught an upper-level pitcher knows that being on the same page as your pitcher is not only important for the team's success, but also for your own physical well-being.

The racial vitriol came from many sources, not just his own teammates and Cap Anson. Upon arriving in Richmond, VA, the Toledo manager Charlie Morton received the following letter: *"Manager Toledo Base Ball Club:*

Dear Sir: We the undersigned, do hereby warn you not to put up Walker, the Negro catcher, the evenings that you play in Richmond, as we could mention the names of 75 determined men who have sworn to mob Walker if he comes to the ground in a suit. We hope you will listen to our words of warning, so that there will be no trouble: but if you do not, there certainly will be.

We only write this to prevent much blood shed, as you alone can prevent." In an era when the justice system was stacked up against people of color, the only real way to avoid this kind of danger was to simply avoid it—by not forcing the issue and engaging in a segregated league rather than trying to push into the White leagues. Fear was a major tactic used by the regressives in fighting against integration, and the power held by Whites in the Jim Crow South meant that these threats were not just empty words, but rather they were true threats to the safety of any person who would dare oppose racial division.

Walker largely avoided conflict and just went about his business as a ballplayer, but eventually he was released by Toledo and never found another Major League level position again. However, he did play some minor league ball for several years, even forming (with George Stovey) the first ever African-American battery in professional baseball history[xxxi]. Stovey, another notable player of the era, was someone who truly lost his opportunity to star in the sport because of the segregation and racism that were so prevalent at the time. Stovey was a considerable talent, hailing from Williamsport, PA (the current home of the Little League World Series and the epicenter of youth baseball in many ways). He was not yet 20 when his talent was beginning to be recognized, and before he was 21 he was hailed as a potential Major League pitcher. Noted sportswriter (and one-time teammate) Sol White said of Stovey, "Were it not for this same man Anson, there would have been a colored player in the National League in 1887[xxxii]." Stovey had a major role in cementing the youth baseball culture in Williamsport, umpiring and organizing youth teams and providing the town with a solid base on which to build the Little League many years later.

Fleet Walker's brief stay in the top tier of professional baseball has become a classic trivia question, but it is rarely seen as being as important as the stories of the men who broke the barriers in 1947 and beyond. However, the importance of Walker's story means it cannot be ignored. Walker represents the end of the reconstruction era in the sport of baseball and the rise of the Jim Crow era. Baseball established its roots in American culture during the Jim Crow era after it was merely a curiosity in Walker's era. When baseball became America's national pastime, it was an ALL WHITE sport. Even when my father grew up in the era of integration, the league really was not welcoming Black players with open arms. In 1947 there were five Black players, two more joined in 1948, four in 1949, and one in 1950, so it was not exactly a flood of new talent. Most players who grew up in the Negro Leagues effectively stayed there. It was about six or seven years *after* Jackie Robinson when most of the league began to embrace Black players.

In the story of Fleet Walker and the 60-year ban on Black players, not everyone in the league sat on the sidelines and did nothing as the league went all-White. Some men, like John McGraw, tried to integrate, but had to attempt to do so through trickery. McGraw was the manager of the Baltimore Orioles back in the early days of the color barrier and in 1901 he signed a man named Charles Grant. However, Grant was light-skinned and McGraw figured it would be easier to get him past the color line if he simply pretended he was a different color than Black. "So, the skipper dressed him up as the Hollywood version of an Indian, face paint and all, according to Black Diamond. Nothing about the get-up was authentic to the Cherokee culture, but that didn't matter. McGraw found the name Tokohama by looking at a map of Hot Springs. It was a nearby creek[xxxiii]." The players on the team seemed fine with the ruse, but Charles Comiskey objected and revealed his true identity. He returned to his Negro League team and never saw another opportunity to play in the MLB. After this attempt, McGraw gave up on his idea of secret integration and the league went another 46 years before seeing Jackie Robinson in a Brooklyn Dodgers uniform.

The history of the color barrier has many villains, but one of them is Tom Yawkey. Despite being an ineffective leader and having limited success, Yawkey was widely celebrated and elected to the Hall of Fame in 1980. This is despite the fact that he never played in an MLB game and never won a championship in over 40 years as owner of the Boston Red Sox. Yawkey literally ran his own team into the ground rather than promote Black players into the Majors. Some said that it was because "Boston would never accept a Black player" and that the city itself was not welcoming to Black players[xxxiv], but since the Boston Braves had integrated without issue, that was simply untrue. In reality, the Red Sox waited until 1959 to add a Black player (Pumpsie Green) to their roster because Yawkey was committed to keeping the Red Sox White.

"The intellectuals invoke muses, angels, and perhaps the devil to explain the ghosts that haunt Fenway. But the simple truth of much of the team's misfortune is more profane: at least until the 1960s, championships eluded the Red Sox because they were committed to bigoted management. Red Sox officials watched while Jackie Robinson, Henry Aaron, Willie Mays, and other Black stars took their teams to another level...they came up short not because they were doomed, but because they were blind to their own interests. During those years, the Red Sox suffered far less from fate than from their front office.[xxxv]" I quote this journal not because I needed the words to be written, but because the journal was written decades ago and not in an era where heroes and prominent figures are receiving new light on their not-so-perfect pasts. It is easy to forget that just a few decades ago it was extremely rare for a person's private feelings on race to be a topic of discussion.

The issue of Tom Yawkey being a racist was well known decades before the Red Sox began to finally distance themselves from his legacy. The Red Sox began to amend for the past by renaming "Yawkey Way" as "Jersey Street", but this was long after he had been referred to as "the biggest bigot in baseball" by Jackie Robinson himself. Again, his legacy was one where the Red Sox never won a championship and at one point had a stretch of eight consecutive losing seasons. The team never got a new stadium in his tenure and the team's attendance numbers suffered for years because of the futility of fielding an all-White team in an integrating league. The Red Sox eventually started winning and drawing fans in large numbers when they were finally utilizing the considerable talents of several Black players to succeed. The Red Sox were an organization that literally chose to lose rather than to move forward with racial relations. Even to this day, Boston has such a reputation for racist fans that many players refuse to play for Boston teams.

"Less than a week after former Major League outfielder Torii Hunter discussed being called the n-word in Boston '100 times,' the Red Sox released a statement Wednesday confirming Hunter's account. 'Torii Hunter's experience is real,' the statement read. 'If you doubt him because you've never heard it yourself, take it from us, it happens." The team said there were seven reported incidents at Fenway Park last season in which fans used racial slurs. 'Those are just the ones we know about. And it's not only players. It happens to the dedicated Black employees who work for us on game days. Their uniforms may be different, but their voices and experiences are just as important.[xxxvi]'" Torii Hunter specifically had a no-trade clause in his contract stating that he would not accept any trade to the Boston Red Sox due to the racism of the fans more than 60 years after Jackie Robinson made his Major League debut. More than 125 years after Fleet Walker was run out of the game of baseball by bigots, men like Torii Hunter were still being made to feel unwelcome to play baseball by the same kinds of people.

CRAWFORD and DPAC

My first full-time high school coaching job was with Crawford High School in San Diego, CA. Crawford had once been one of the traditional powers of the old city league decades before, but had long since fallen upon hard times as a baseball program. More than 15 years had passed since Crawford had a winning season, and in that period there had been seasons of 3-23, 2-18, 0-16, 3-20 (twice), 0-24, 1-24 (the only win was by forfeit), 0-18, and 1-23 (again, the only win was by forfeit). That's five seasons in 15 years where the baseball team at Crawford never actually won a baseball game. When I joined the program, it was in the midst of a losing streak that we ended at 46 games. In the two years following my departure, the program lost all 41 games it played.

If you were a baseball player entering high school, would you join a program with that kind of record? As a result, Crawford's program has no incoming ballplayers and a ton of attrition because a lot of kids will not take those kinds of defeats over and over again very well. Within the Central League, there is a lot of animosity between kids at the various schools, and much of it is gang related. These traditional Central League programs are Crawford, Hoover, San Diego High School, Lincoln, Kearny, and Morse, though the league changes slightly each year. One year the Central League contained Clairemont and Mission Bay and that led to the Crawford team losing a game 38-0 to Mission Bay in just 2.5 innings before having to come back to the same field the next day to play the same team again. To get the kids to come to the second game, I had to promise to buy them all dinner after the game. I literally used 10% of my team's budget for the whole year to buy them all Thai food because only one player on the team had ever experienced that kind of cuisine. I figured they might as well make a positive memory on a day when they had to go back to a field to suffer another humiliating defeat with no chance for victory. In fact, I spent more than half my budget on meals for my players either because they could not afford dinner after our games or because

I needed something to motivate them to return to a field where they had suffered a humiliating loss. More equipment would not have made an impact, because my players simply did not have the experience or personal training resources to compete anyway, so meals carried more value to the kids than a new bat or glove.

Maybe you're thinking the records are the whole picture. Maybe the games were competitive but the Crawford Colts simply couldn't eke out the close ones. Well, you would be wrong if you thought that. For the years 2015–2019, Crawford scored 87 runs total and gave up 1167 in league play. Yes, that's less than 100 runs scored while giving up more than 1000. The four main other teams in the league (Morse, Kearny, Lincoln, and Hoover) all had positive run differentials in the same period, and if you combined all the runs given up by those four teams, they would still total 10 fewer than Crawford did on its own. Lincoln, which was only in the league in 3 of the 5 years, still scored 193 more runs in Central League play in that period than

Crawford. Why would anyone want to play on a team where the average score of every game is Crawford 1, Opponents 19? Crawford scored 87 runs in total in five years—not five *games*, five *years*. Mission Bay High School scored 69 runs in 5 innings against Crawford in 2017 (they were a league opponent for that season), whereas Crawford took three YEARS to score that many runs.

Racial demographics in the Central League are relatively similar, so the real difference is seen in the number of students living in poverty. Kearny has about 75% of its students on free/reduced-price lunch, Morse is around 80%, Lincoln is around 85%, and Hoover and Crawford are generally over 90%. Interestingly enough, the order of their success in league is directly correlated to the poverty levels of their students. As a school's poverty rate decreases, their success increases. For a comparison, the top program in the central San Diego area (Point Loma High School) has only 35% of its students on free/reduced-price lunches. Other top programs in the San

Diego Unified school district include Scripps Ranch (15%), La Jolla (23%), and University City (40%), and some of the top teams in the section are Eastlake (22%), Poway (26%), and Sage Creek (18%). No top ten program is over 60%, but nearly all of the bottom ten programs sit at that level or significantly higher[xxxvii]. This mirrors the shift of baseball more and more towards wealthy, suburban neighborhoods. "Inner-city baseball numbers have shot down for years, while club numbers are going up," said Jerry Schniepp, the CIF-San Diego Section Commissioner and former baseball coach at Helix. "It's a pay-to-play thing. It creates a high level of competition in baseball in some areas, which is why San Diego is so competitive with the rest of the country...But the inner cities struggle with that. It's not like basketball, where you can grab a ball and get on the court. It requires a lot of equipment and money for competition[xxxviii]."

Things with Crawford had gotten so bad that the San Diego Union Tribune used my team in an exposé of the disparities in San Diego high school baseball.

"It takes only one visit to a Crawford game to understand how far a quality program can crumble under the weight of changing times. On an overcast afternoon last week, the Colts hosted Clairemont on a Colina Park del Sol community field that is a couple blocks from campus in City Heights. They lost 16-0. 'One of our best games,' head coach Dan Pasternack said. More squirrels than spectators flitted around the old concrete stands. The all-dirt infield was a finger painting of browns because a city work crew hastily dragged over it. There were no lines on the field, Pasternack

offered, because the chalker 'vanished.' There are no outfield fences because the school shares the field with various soccer programs. That was unfortunate in one game because Crawford might have had its only home run of the season, but a soccer player picked up the live ball and threw it back. On the low-slung dugout benches sat 11 uniformed players. About 40 signed up for baseball, Pasternack said, but nearly half of those never got medical clearance. Sixteen started the year, and the squad's numbers have dwindled as the season, and losing, wore on. Kids become ineligible because of grades. Others *can only show up sporadically because they have jobs. Two boys, Pasternack said, were nearly homeless, and saved only by living with friends. One student's brother was deported, the coach said, and other players worried that they would be picked up by immigration officers during practice. 'These kids have different worries,' Pasternack said. 'We played Clairemont. Their biggest worry is, am I going to get to practice on time? Or is my mom going to buy me that $450 bat?'"xxxix*

Kids of privilege simply do not understand the struggle that kids at schools like Crawford have to go through. Worrying about whether or not you can ever see your brother again or wondering if you will have a place to sleep tonight is certainly going to take precedence over a sport that does not even really welcome you as a player. At one point later that season, I had three players who were no longer living with their families, one of whom was fully supporting himself, and an additional player who was effectively living on his own due to the fact that his parents were still living in Africa and he was merely staying with a distant relative in San Diego.

Crawford High School sits in a neighborhood which has become one of the poorest in San Diego and which is home to a large number of refugees and immigrants from countries where baseball does not have any kind of presence. The school is one where only 19% of the students speak English as a first language (Point Loma High School has over 75%) and where just 12.6% of the kids are classified as "gifted," compared to the 39% at Point Loma. Additionally, more than 33% of Crawford students come from a family where their parents are not high school graduates, compared to just 4% at Point Loma[xl]. Because of the cost of baseball, this demographic data at Crawford is extremely telling. Based on those numbers, it is next to impossible for Crawford to have a successful baseball program in a city like San Diego. How can a kid afford to become a strong baseball player when their parents are likely struggling to put food on the table and a roof over their heads?

Because of the struggles of the program and the economic realities of baseball, tryouts at Crawford may have a large number of interested potential players, but few of them have any prior baseball experience. Year in, year out, the program suffers humiliating defeats with 20+ run margins. Many kids quit the program throughout the season as the blowout losses pile up and the program pretty much has to restart from scratch each season. Despite this, it is one of the most historically significant baseball programs in the city with 19 players drafted in the 1970s and 1980s and eight who made it to the Major Leagues, making it historically one of the top 10 programs in San Diego[xli]. As a result, this history causes the old guard of the San Diego high school baseball leadership to assume Crawford can "return to its glory days," because none of those administrators has any concept of what it would take to achieve that.

Each year at the coaches meeting, the Crawford coach makes a plea to be moved down into a league with baseball programs at a more appropriate level for the Colts, and each year they are forced to remain in their traditional league with the other central San Diego high schools, where they have no chance for success. No team should remain in a league where it is outscored by an average of 18 runs a game, especially when you consider that many of those games end after just 2.5–4.5 innings due to the mercy rule. Despite the clear evidence that Crawford and Kearny simply do not belong in the same league, they spend year after year wasting time and money on games where the outcome is known the moment the game shows up on the schedule: Kearny def. Crawford (mercy rule). Crawford has played some close games, but those were against programs from similar situations, like King-Chavez or Gompers Prep, where few of the players have any travel ball experience. Success against similar programs will help keep some neighborhood kids from playing elsewhere or playing a different sport, because Crawford will not have a reputation of losing every game by 20.

Many people think that a great coach can just turn any weak program into a powerhouse, but it takes more than coaching. Back in the 1950s, all that mattered was that your school was in a neighborhood with a youth league, but these days the elite programs poach players from other schools until one school has such a weak program that no serious baseball players would ever consider going there. Coaching in baseball can only go so far. Baseball is a skill-based sport, and it takes years to develop those skills. To build a successful baseball program from scratch at a school in a poor neighborhood is nearly impossible: Not only do you need to have a ton of money to have proper training equipment, balls, bats, gloves, etc., but you also need to be able to bring experienced players to the program. Recruiting becomes the only avenue in which a program can rise from doormat to respectable. The problem with baseball, however, is that the kids who would be quality recruits at the high school level are generally from well off families (or at least middle class), and they have no desire to attend an inner-city school just to help improve the baseball program.

Another issue holding back schools like Crawford is that you also need a large coaching staff to truly be able to compete with wealthier programs, where having 6+ adults working at practice is commonplace. Budgets at elite programs are upwards of $50,000, and sometimes over $100,000. Budgets for programs like Crawford are $3,000–$5,000 for everything. You cannot build a coaching staff when all you can pay assistants is $500 for a whole high school season. Kids at rich schools not only already have all their own equipment (I have provided gloves, bats, balls, batting gloves, baseball pants, athletic protectors, etc. to my players at poor high schools), they also have their own coaches. I grew up with a pitching coach and a hitting coach who both had extensive Major League experience, but most players at low-income schools have never had personal coaches. The teams themselves can afford to pay for extra coaching, too, by adding all kinds of experienced coaches to their staffs. I have coached solo for large chunks of seasons and while I consider myself an effective coach, I simply am incapable of providing quality practices without someone to throw batting practice, someone to hit flies, someone to hit grounders, and someone to work with hitters while I do bullpen sessions with my pitchers. Coaching solo is very common for low budget programs, and without a real budget to pay assistants, the ones I do hire are usually unreliable or not committed enough to make any kind of impact. A team of 18 kids needs a coaching staff of at least three to have any effectiveness, and to compete it probably requires six or more coaches.

When I coach by myself, I have to essentially do one of two things: have all the kids doing the same drill together with me, or send them off to attempt to do drills on their own. The problem with this is that they may not be able to do the drill properly or they may goof off without adult supervision.

Teenagers will be teenagers, and the overwhelming majority of them are not committed enough to practice when the coach isn't looking. Sure, they will play and do baseball stuff, but the seriousness that a coach brings generally is not replicated by a group of players. Even Major League teams have coaching staffs of more than a half dozen, and those are the best, most committed players in the world. Kids with no experience and limited skills need all the coaching they can get.

While coaching at Crawford my teams were not completely devoid of talent. I actually had a couple of pretty decent players there, but one player stood out among the rest, so I made it my goal to get his career to continue beyond the sandlot field of Colina Del Sol park. This kid, Mabele Sapili, was originally from The Congo in Central Africa and had never seen baseball before he started high school. One day he was playing soccer and saw one of my friends (Quinn Mayfield), a baseball coach, hitting some ground balls to his players, so he ran over to inquire about the game they were playing. It looked like fun to him, so he decided to give it a try. It was not long before he was able to track a ball, run it down, and secure it in his glove. Soon he was able to throw the ball and started to pick up some skills at the plate. I started coaching him as a senior and it was obvious that he was something special. Sapili was the best player on the team by far and after every game the opposing coach would talk to me about him and his other-worldly range in the outfield. He would often attempt to catch foul popups—from center field—and everyone on the field's jaw would drop. Because of his obvious talent, I decided to use $750 of my own money to let him show off his skills in a Perfect Game showcase.

At the Showcase, there were about 200 players, all elite and high-level performers on the field. Sapili was the least experienced and the one from the weakest high school program. By far. He was also completely out of his element in a structured scout camp environment when many of his peers had been going to them 4–5 times a year for half a decade. He acted like he was practicing at first, so I had to take him aside and tell him, "You have to show off. You need to stand out—make them notice you". He started off on his 60-yard dash in a jog, but then realized he needed to kick into gear and sped up and completed the sprint in a time that put him among the elites despite the slow start. I was watching him and a couple of gentlemen approached me. One was from City College of San Diego and the other from the Seattle Mariners. They both expressed interest in him and he eventually went to City College. Unfortunately, he suffered a leg injury and never got the chance to play college ball, but the opportunity was there. I moved away from San Diego in 2017 and went to start a program at a new charter high school in Las Vegas. At Democracy Prep at the Agassi Campus (DPAC), despite many astronomical challenges, I have had a few quality ballplayers who had the chance to play at the next level.

One of my first players at DPAC with the next-level ability/talent was Jordan Jourdain, an undersized but extremely athletic utility player. Jordan grew up with an interest in baseball, but never really did much with it until I started the program at DPAC. He was my captain and most motivated player, and he had a really bright future on the field. Unfortunately Jordan suffered a traumatic brain injury during the summer between his junior and senior years[xlii] and nearly died. He spent several months recovering and still got back on the field for his senior year, but he had some pretty heavy rust as a result of having to learn how to walk again. After a month or so of practice, he began to recover his ability but he definitely saw a drop in his production compared to what he could have done without such a rocky start. Jordan would have been working out daily (that is how he got injured in the first place, he was doing indoor workouts to avoid Las Vegas summertime heat and had a freak accident in the gym which caused him to hit a brick wall head on) and had a serious chance to shine his senior year. Nevertheless, he did have a strong enough season to get some NAIA offers, but had Jordan been raised with money in a stable environment, who knows how much of an impact that would have had on him? Jordan has superior physical tools compared to most kids who get drafted every year, but he simply lacks the experience, consistency, or skill level to outshine those kids who go to every showcase in the region and get on scouts radars when they are 13 years old.

I have had a few other players at DPAC with this type of potential, but the other challenge I face is the pull of other sports. Ramon Green was a very similar player to Jordan Jourdain, but unlike Jordan, he was not taken by the game of baseball in the same way. He was a football player at heart, and instead of focusing on baseball, a sport where his elite athleticism and superior hand-eye coordination (he batted over .400 his senior year and was among the state leaders in stolen bases) would let him shine, he chose to pursue football opportunities. Ramon could have been a high level baseball player, but instead followed a different path. Micah Gayman, Ramon's teammate on the football team, was a different kind of player, but also a college-level baseball talent. He allowed football to take not only his heart but also his body. Micah was the quarterback of the football team and had an elite arm. He also had legitimate power at the plate and enough speed to bat over .400 and be one of the state leaders in stolen bases and triples as a junior. Micah did not get to play as a senior because he had a devastating knee injury from his senior football season and the Covid-19 virus put a stop to the baseball season before he was cleared by his doctor to return to activity. Had Micah focused on baseball instead of football, he would have easily been throwing 90+ miles per hour and hitting over .500 as a senior.

Because of the inner-city's focus on football and basketball, most potential baseball stars do not grow up in the game. Many kids may play a bit of Little League, but most leave the sport well before they are old enough to truly develop any baseball skills. They focus on other sports and generally leave baseball behind. Some return to the sport in high school, but by that time their peers in the suburbs have played hundreds of travel ball games. Herein lies the problem with inner-city programs. Baseball is a sport that requires a lot of time to excel more than your peers. Sheer physical talent helps—a lot—but it is still insufficient to make up for missing out on years of practice and hundreds of games/innings. While players at DPAC and Crawford get about 100 innings a season (at best), most of them do *not* get any additional game experience in a year. Kids at Rancho Bernardo, Arbor View, or Serra, on the other hand, play about 250 regular season innings and another several hundred in travel ball and showcases, and they do that for years. Just four years of that disparity means kids from DPAC or Crawford likely have 1,000 fewer innings of high school level baseball. Add in the fact that showcases cost anywhere from $300-$1,000+ and you can see how the lower-income kids get pushed aside. For this situation to improve, much stronger rules need to be in place in high school ball for poaching players districted to other programs, and budgets need to be equalized more. These are both extremely controversial ideas, however, and the powers-that-be would fight tooth-and-nail against such drastic changes.

In reality, high school sports as a whole are dying as a springboard to the pros as the travel ball circuits grow in power and influence. High school basketball stars bounce around the country from school to school so they can play on the best AAU team to get exposure. Jaden Agassi, the son of the successful pro tennis players Steffi Graf and Andre Agassi, proved that playing high school baseball is unnecessary to gain college scholarships or to be on the top prospects list. He barely played any games in his high school career and yet ended up as a scholarship athlete at the University of Southern California, one of the best baseball programs in the country. He was ranked the #1 third baseman in the state of Nevada and the #13 nationally, all despite barely playing any high school games[xliii]. Football is slightly different because of the large budget necessary to run a program, but many other sports have long since abandoned high school as the primary springboard to next-level success. This does not change the fact that poor schools will continue to suffer humiliating defeats until leagues start to make attempts to normalize competition somewhat. Based on the coaches meetings I have attended in Little League, and at high schools in San Diego and Las Vegas, I can say for a fact that there is not any kind of motivation to make any changes to improve competitive balance because all that matters to most coaches is that they win the championship by any means necessary.

ATHLETIC INITIATIVE

I met April and Rich Curry through my involvement in Old Town Academy, a K–8 charter school in San Diego. One of my first times seeing Rich in action, he was yelling at some corporate guys about how they were forcing kids off of a recreation center's basketball court. The corporate guys had reserved the court and were clearly not hurting for money if the Ferrari in the parking lot was any indication. Rich went way over the top in his reaction, but I knew right then that he was my kind of person. We immediately became close friends. Rich and I were two peas in a pod: Our vision for the world and how we see education and athletics were right in line with each other and we quickly became partners in a nonprofit organization he founded (Athletic Initiative, Inc.,) with his wife April. April reminded me of my sister, so the three of us knew that we should be more than just colleagues from the charter school. I joined their nonprofit board as the Treasurer and we began a journey into the depths of youth baseball in San Diego. My sister connected me to someone at the San Diego Padres and I was able to arrange a meeting with them to see about getting Athletic Initiative involved in their community programs. After some hard work by April and Rich, we were able to get the Padres to sign off on us becoming their official partners for the RBI (Reviving Baseball in Inner Cities) program.

For those unfamiliar with the RBI program, it is designed to fight the main problem this book is all about. First, a little history about the RBI Program: As a scout for the Detroit Tigers after his playing career was over, John Young noticed a lack of African-American prospects. While working for the Baltimore Orioles, he surveyed prospects selected in the 1986 MLB Draft, many of whom attended four-year colleges, and then noticed that among California colleges, only 4% of players were African-American and less than 3% were Hispanic. He presented his findings to Orioles' general manager Roland Hemond and MLB Commissioner Peter Ueberroth. Ueberroth contacted Tom Bradley, the mayor of Los Angeles, who agreed to fund a youth baseball program in Los Angeles, providing $50,000^{xliv}$. This seed money helped to build RBI's flagship program and the model in which most other urban baseball programs followed thereafter.

RBI has a noble goal, but has it really been effective? The percentage of African-American players on Opening Day rosters dropped from 19% in 1995 to 8.5% in 2013, a period when the RBI program was fully active. Does this mean that RBI has been an abject failure? Probably not. But it does point to the fact that the problem in baseball's ever-shifting demographics is more than just opportunity to play the game. The main weakness of the RBI mission is that it does nothing to prepare players for the modern era of baseball, where athletes specialize and have year-round travel ball, clinics, and camps to hone their skills. RBI still caters to kids who cannot afford to play elite baseball and as a result, does little to bridge the gap between the haves and have-nots.

In running the RBI program in San Diego, we saw the

challenges first-hand. With our leagues, any kid with any kind of baseball experience was a dominant force who could shift the balance of a game significantly by themselves. I ran the oldest division and turned the 18U team into a travel team because there were not enough players to create an in-house league. We played mostly low-income high school programs and similar travel teams in the San Diego area. Our biggest asset was the fact that I had a key to a private baseball field and the ability to hold practices at my convenience, which is a luxury most inner-city programs simply do not have. My team was quite successful, but it was more because I had used my connections to players from previous leagues I had coached in and built an all-star team of experienced ballplayers. However, as a whole program, we struggled to gain much traction in building elite baseball players because one practice a week and one two-hour game on the weekend is simply not enough to catch up to kids who are practicing three days and playing the other four every week. Sure, my team was successful, and we got plenty of kids interested in the game, but none of the elite high school programs were fed by our leagues.

This is why RBI has not been successful in its mission despite trying to do all the right things. RBI deserves to survive and exist, but for it to make any kind of discernible impact on the demographics of Major League Baseball it needs to expand significantly and adjust to the times. Sure, in 1994 it was possible for a kid to make the majors just from playing some ball part time, but those days are long gone. In 2020 a kid needs to be focused 100% on baseball from a young age to have a shot at ever making it to the next level unless that kid is an absolutely elite athlete who makes all-state in multiple sports. You simply will not see a kid who plays 20 games and practices for just 3–4 months a year make the Majors without some kind of other-worldly talent.

I love the mission of RBI, but why has it failed to really bring any change to the trends in baseball demographics in America? One major factor is the noncompetitive nature of the leagues and teams. There are some competitive RBI teams and leagues, but most are purely recreational and they do not push for any development beyond the program. You do not see many RBI programs sponsoring elite travel teams; instead, they stick to segregated leagues in poor neighborhoods with limited coaching and cheap equipment, and that is not a springboard to an elite high school team, let alone the Major Leagues. You just do not see elite baseball players at scout camps using plastic gloves or hand-me-down equipment like you see on the RBI fields. It is a great program to maybe influence the next generation of baseball parents, but not as a tool to improve racial and economic diversity in the game of baseball.

To be able to excel in any sport, an athlete needs to have the opportunity to push themselves beyond their capabilities. Distance runners do not just quit their training runs at exactly their competition distance and pole vaulters do not just keep jumping at their maximum level. Instead, they go beyond what they have ever done before to challenge their strength, stamina, skill, technique, etc. Players who want to reach the NFL have to face NFL quality opponents to be able to show that they are capable. Basketball players gain notoriety not for having 50-point games against overmatched opponents, but for holding their own against already established prospects. Mikey Williams, for example, became one of the most prominent basketball prospects in the country after he played in a tournament in the DPAC gym. His teammate was LeBron "Bronny" James, Jr., so there was a massive media presence for the games and a lot of celebrities who wanted to see Bronny play. Lebron even gave the crowd the pleasure of some showoff dunks during warm-ups, but when the games started it was Mikey Williams, not Bronny James, who got all the attention. Mikey was already established as a strong prospect before that tournament, but his star took off after it. Williams dominated as a freshman in high school, but it was his experience on the travel circuit and his dominance of heavily scouted talents that truly cemented his place on the map.

A huge problem facing high school sports is that far too many people think that playing sports will lead to a lucrative professional career. Even in the most niche sports, where only a handful of people participate, this just is not the case. There are about 125,000 players per grade in high school baseball, but of those 125,000, how many are actually destined to play professionally? Basically none, because there are less than 10,000 total professional ballplayers at all levels, where many come from outside the country and range in age from 16 to 40-something. If as many as 10% of the total ballplayers in any given year are from the same high school class year, then there are 1000 pros (this means all levels, not just MLB, which is only a small portion of the professional players in MLB systems) from each grade level. Then, based on that, roughly 1 out of every 125 high school players make it to the pro ranks, and even fewer make it to the Major Leagues. Moreover, those players are heavily concentrated in specific programs, so the odds are even steeper for players from outside those powerhouses.

The leagues I have coached in at the high school level have all had about 6–8 teams, which amounts to ~125 players. So, from those leagues, only one player is likely to ever play professionally each year and it is usually pretty obvious who that one kid is. There may be years when three or four kids from a lower level league may make it, but then there will also be years or even decades where players from that league never make it. Conversely, elite baseball schools like Bishop Gorman High School in Las Vegas have players drafted frequently. In fact, Bishop Gorman has a streak of 16 straight seasons where an alumnus of their program was drafted in addition to the four or five players who go to NCAA Division 1 programs. So, keeping those numbers in mind, the chance for kids becoming professional baseball players from the lower divisions of baseball in Nevada is far lower than 1/125. So who are the kids that play at Bishop Gorman? They are travel ball players who have the means to pay for camps, clinics, private coaches, and a team with a staff of at least a half-dozen coaches.

If more people realized that playing professionally is not in the cards, the competitiveness of high school ball would likely fade back to the way it was before everyone thought their ticket to wealth was through playing sports. High school sports should be competitive, but not at the expense of the game itself. Baseball is becoming more of a niche sport in part because too many parents think their little Johnny is the next Mike Trout when he's really just the next "guy who used to play baseball back in high school," so they invest heavily in their child, which encourages other parents to invest even more in theirs. This continuous escalation has priced many athletes out of what used to be America's Pastime.

Many of today's best athletes are either the kids of great athletes (Patrick Mahomes, Stephen Curry, Fernando Tatis, Jr., Bo Bichette, Vlad Guerrero, Jr., the Bosa Brothers) or kids of great privilege who grow up with private coaches, travel ball showcases, and parents who literally put their personal and professional lives on the line to help hone their children's' skills (the Ball Brothers, Kris Bryant, the Watt Brothers), or in reality, a little bit of both. Outside of the US these standards may be a bit different, but here in the US it takes time, money, and transportation to make it in sports. This isn't to say that it is impossible to make it without these advantages, but rather that to make it you have to beat out people with those advantages. This is why the inner-city kid who gets to the Majors is such an anomaly these days, because even a talented and highly motivated kid without advantages is likely to get left in the dust by their more privileged peers.

TERRY WHITFIELD

Terry Whitfield is not a household name, but he was a heck of a hitter in the Major Leagues and the Japanese Pacific League for most of the 1970s and 1980s. Terry's career batting average was .281 in MLB, .286 in the Minor Leagues, and .289 in Japan. He was never a superstar in the States, but in his three seasons in Japan, he was named to the league's "Best Nine" twice, and he was the best player on the best team in the league in 1983. Terry's career was not too much of a struggle once he reached the professional ranks, but getting there took a ton of hard work. He did not grow up with wealth and privilege like some of his peers, but his family played a major role in helping him develop into a Major Leaguer. His father worked as a janitor and provided Terry with whatever he needed through hard work and dedication and those values transferred to Terry as a young child and well into his life as one of the most respected baseball people in the San Francisco Bay Area in the 1990s.

Whitfield was not just a great baseball player—he was a

standout in football and basketball as well. While he was growing up, Terry thought he would actually play football at the next level, but after being drafted by the Yankees in the first round, he was given the opportunity to be a top baseball player. As a young first-round pick, Terry's experience in the early 1970s was split between the Deep South and Upstate New York. He spent time in Tennessee, North Carolina, and Florida and dealt with some major challenges due to his race, but he also got to experience the best of Minor League Baseball in small town New York, where he was welcomed like family.

While playing in the Florida State League (single-A ball, the lowest level of the Minors), Terry was one of only a few Black players on his team and he dealt with some pretty serious racial discrimination. He had to live in a hotel with the other two Black players because no apartments in the city would rent to them. They would be told by White teammates that there was a quality apartment available for rent, but when Terry and his teammates showed up, the vacancy would suddenly be "filled".

Terry and his two Black teammates eventually became stressed out by the living situation and began to argue with each other regularly. Because of the challenges with housing, the frustration of being isolated from the rest of the team wore on all three of them, and Terry suffered through the worst season of his career at any level. He batted just .163 in 49 games and his potential to reach MLB was starting to look suspect.

For many players, that struggle in A ball would have been the end of their MLB dreams, but it was different for Terry because he had been a first-round pick. The Yankees sent him to Oneonta, NY, with another Black player named Larry Murray. Oneonta is a small city of about 15,000 residents that sits roughly a half hour south of the Baseball Hall of Fame in Cooperstown, NY. Oneonta is not a diverse city and has never been one, but it was a much more tolerant and accepting city for Terry and Larry in 1972. Both Terry and Larry had struggled mightily in Florida that year, but both thrived in Oneonta. Terry started becoming an extra-base-hit machine and Larry became a prolific base stealer. To think that these two young ballplayers could both go from batting below .165 to being two of the most dangerous players in the league simply from moving into a more welcoming environment, it makes you wonder how many ballplayers suffered a different fate and saw their careers dry up as a result. In Terry's words, "We got shipped to NY and it changed my life. They treated us well, bought us dinners for home runs and stuff. You didn't make that much money at that time, so it helped a lot.[xlv]" If not for his experience in Oneonta, who knows what would have happened to Terry Whitfield.

The next season Whitfield went to play in the Carolina League for the Kinston Eagles at the tender age of 20. The Carolina League (High-A Ball) was mostly guys around 22–23 years old and Terry was one of the five youngest hitters in the whole league. His youth did not mean he was overmatched by the league, however. Terry actually was the only hitter under the age of 23 to bat over .300 and was the league leader in batting average, home runs, and on base percentage; he was also one of the top two in the league in hits, runs scored, doubles, and slugging percentage, and he was fourth in RBIs. Terry was proving to be an elite hitter, especially considering that he was so much younger than nearly everyone in the league. His success on the field did not mean, however, that he was immune to discrimination off the field. "I wanted to get a place close to the ballpark with a couple guys. But when I came down the stairs on the first morning there, there was a guy across the street with a shotgun. This was 1973 and it was still not an integrated neighborhood. I started hitting the ball just to get the heck out of there, so I won the batting title." At the end of the season when Terry was leaving town, the woman who rented him his apartment said to him "Terry, Boy, I thought you was gonna be something else. You turned out to be a good boy". This is a perfect example of a "micro-aggression", a comment or action that subtly and often unconsciously or unintentionally expresses a prejudiced attitude toward a member of a traditionally oppressed group.

For Terry's story, not all the White people with power were villains. One of the most polarizing figures in baseball history played a major role in Terry's rise to the Majors. George Steinbrenner was always a fan of Terry's and helped in his ascent. "Steinbrenner was the one guy that always liked me. Everything he did, he took care of me, and that's one thing I'm really grateful for." Steinbrenner was a man who was known for his sometimes ruthless style of management, but he also had a huge heart and a desire to help those in need. When Darryl Strawberry was in the midst of a major struggle with substance abuse and teetering on the brink of losing his career, Steinbrenner stepped up to help him. "I know about all the problems he's had, but he was a young man who was important to baseball at one point," Steinbrenner said. "In my mind, I wonder if he can be important to baseball again…But equally important, his life still has a lot to go ahead of it. And if I can be a help to a young man like that, I want to do it. And I want to stand with him as he attempts to overcome certain things[xlvi]."

This aspect of Steinbrenner's personality is often forgotten when the Yankees owner is the topic of discussion.

After his big season in Carolina, Terry played the 1974 season for the Syracuse Chiefs of the International League. The International League was a AAA program, so Terry skipped the AA level entirely. At the time it was a pitcher-dominated league and Terry had a decent, but not spectacular season. He struck out more than any other hitter in the league by a wide margin and was caught stealing 9 times in just 15 tries. He did end up a top-6 home run hitter and was second in doubles, so the power and hitting ability were still there, but it was not an ideal season for him. That said, he was still one of the youngest players in the league and his success caught the attention of the big league club. "When I got sent home in September, Steinbrenner called me and said, 'Get on a plane and come here to New York and get here before gametime'". That was the beginning of Terry's Major League career and on September 29, 1974, he made his Major League debut at the age of 21.

Terry bounced between AAA and the Majors the next couple of seasons before being traded to San Francisco to join the Giants as a full-time Major League outfielder. Terry spent four years with the Giants, played 514 games, and established himself as an integral part of the franchise during the late 1970s. He hit .289 in his career with the Giants, a stat which places him in the top 40 all-time in an organization with 138 years of history (from 1883 to 2020)[xlvii]. Despite that success, the Giants sent Whitfield to the Seibu Lions in Japan before the 1981 season. Whitfield believed the move to be as a result of some discrimination within the Giants organization: "There were some incidents where there was obviously blatant prejudice, but I just wanted to play. When an opportunity came up, they refused to trade me, but then this thing came up with Japan, so they chose to send me to Japan instead of sending me to an opponent[xlviii]." Terry was 28 years old and an established Major League star when he went to Japan. The move would prove to be a challenge, but one that benefitted Whitfield greatly.

"I was 28 years old when I went to Japan. That was probably the best thing that ever happened to me. Over there I was a Gaijin, you will never be accepted and will never be a real Japanese player." Because Terry was finally seen as an equal to every other American ballplayer and was seen just for his production, he was able to settle into his role more. He began to establish himself in Japan as a strong hitter and also started giving back to the community more, often inviting local kids to the games. Terry's first year in Japan was successful, but he began to struggle in his second season with Seibu. What happened next mirrors the popular film "Mr. Baseball" so much that it nearly feels as though Tom Selleck's character was based on Whitfield.

"We had a manager who was like 'God Almighty' and he destroyed a lot of people's lives. One day it was raining and he wanted us to do some running. 'I can pull my hamstring,' I said and the manager still forced me to run in the rain and sure enough I pulled my hamstring and the manager fined me $5,000. I was having a terrible year and I started to go to a person in Japan who taught me about how to breathe, relax, settle down. 'To be successful in Japan, you gotta allow yourself to fail,' he said to me. I apologized to my manager even though I knew it wasn't the way I would do it, but it was how it was done in Japan and he accepted. He then had me get this deep massage. The hitting coach said, 'Terry, you don't know nothing.' 'One who doesn't know nothing is ready to learn.' I learned so much from him about hitting, how to use my body, etc. That understanding that sometimes we gotta give up our pride to actually learn. If I didn't do that, I would've been stuck and not moved forward." These lessons Terry learned in Japan were invaluable not only to him (the next season Whitfield hit 38 home runs and was one of the best players in Japan), but also to the generations of ballplayers he influenced along the way.

Coach Terry, as I knew him growing up, spent many years in Burlingame, CA, running FuturePro, where he had a batting cage and put on clinics and camps. He hosted birthday parties and he opened his doors to anyone that wanted to get better at baseball. He not only exposed many White ballplayers to the experience of having a Black coach, but also opened their eyes to the values of the techniques taught in Japan. Terry also created a training device called the "Terry Toss" that even 25 years later has yet to be replicated—I know because I have tried for years to get an equivalent device for my own teams, and all have come up miles short of the value of the "Terry Toss". Unfortunately, Terry watched as his son struggled to make his way in baseball. "My son was told, 'You're not playing because you're Black' but I couldn't speak up because my son wouldn't let me." One time when Terry's son was injured on the field and Terry ran out to take care of him, the coach came out and accused his son of "playing around". This is a perfect example of the implicit bias Black people often face when dealing with pain management or emergency situations.

Terry Whitfield is not a legendary player. They do not make baseball cards of his as special inserts in 2021 Topps packs. He is not the subject of any documentaries or bestselling biographies. But Coach Terry had an impact that has ripples across all of Major League Baseball to this day. Numerous Major League players used his camps to hone their skills and many more took cuts in his cages and took pitching lessons with the various members of the coaching staff. Often we would be hitting in the cage when a current member of the Giants would saunter in and just hang out with Terry. It was obvious that he was respected across the generations of baseball. For me, I certainly could not imagine my life without FuturePro and Terry Whitfield, and I am pretty sure that there are hundreds or even thousands of other Bay Area baseball players who feel the same way. But this impact is only apparent to those who truly experienced it, so as far as I know, this book is one of the few places to truly celebrate it.

Herein lies the problem with measuring impact: Terry has done a ton for the game of baseball and had a direct impact on many Major League players, but that impact never gets mentioned when watching MLB broadcasts. Everyone knows Jackie Robinson, many know Larry Doby, but few know of Hank Thompson or Willard Brown. The first person to do something is lauded as a hero and receives press for their accomplishment. The second may receive some recognition, but they always receive far less fanfare than the first. The third and fourth generally receive little recognition, despite often facing many of the same challenges the first couple people faced. In the end, people like Terry Whitfield never receive full recognition because people do not put in the effort to celebrate everyone, just those who make the most recognizable impact.

ICEMAN AND FRENCHIE

This section is about two players of mine who played on the same team in San Diego. I call one of them Iceman and the other Frenchie (nicknames I gave them) to protect their anonymity, but I'm pretty sure anyone who knows me or these kids will be well aware of who they are. Frenchie was a very troubled kid from a foster home who had finally found some stability. He was extremely high energy and certainly had his moments of immaturity, but he was a strong player and his teammates loved him. He was also a highly coachable kid who had clearly never received any coaching prior to playing on my team. He improved greatly during the season and was, without question, the player who would rise to the competition the most. The better the pitching, the better he would hit. The harder the play in the field, the more likely it was he would make it. He had speed, power, could play anywhere in the field and was not intimidated by hard throwers. He was a clear all-star, not just because his statistics warranted it (I always keep extremely detailed stats), but because he truly was one of the players who would excel most in all-star play.

Iceman was an extremely quiet kid. You might think he didn't speak English from the way he carried himself. I coached him as a rising 13-year-old through the time he was about 17. He was the most coachable kid I have ever had. I put him on the mound one day and by the end of the bullpen session he had the best cutter and slider of any kid I had ever coached. He was simply the consummate ballplayer. I had him behind the plate, at shortstop, centerfield, third base—it really didn't matter. He would play anywhere I put him and do it with a smile. He was a solid pitcher and an excellent hitter. He basically never got caught stealing (and I stole a lot at that level) and was truly the epitome of an all-star. He was also quite tanned and came from a modest background with a quiet and humble family. His father was always there to cheer him on, but never once uttered a word to coaches about playing time, positions or anything else. That made it difficult to stand out at that Little League, where the president ruled with an iron fist and did whatever it took to put his own children's interests ahead of everyone else's.

The league president was the epitome of everything I associate with what is wrong with Little League. His entire goal was to create the perfect avenue for his kids to shine, even if it was at the expense of every other child. He became president, not to help all the kids, but to help his own. When I joined the board, I continually made suggestions to improve competitive balance and opportunities for the kids whose parents were not as involved and I was shut down every time. When I took over the Juniors division and made sure to divide the players into three perfectly even teams to ensure fair competition, he literally snuck his kid onto one of the teams with two games before the playoffs when his son's high school season ended. He then overruled two nominations to the all-star team, Iceman and Frenchie (who was Black), in favor of his own son (not an all-star by any stretch of the imagination) and another well-off White kid who was on my roster (and was not even in my top six players). The all-star team for a league with ~40 players was nearly all White, despite the league being quite diverse. This was by design.

By selecting mostly White kids year after year for all-star play, it creates a systematic exclusion for the advancement of Black and Brown players. If a kid is selected for all-stars from age 8–14 and played in the same exact leagues as a kid who was not selected, the all-star player will have played at least 25 more games (and likely upwards of 50 or 100+ if they come from an elite league) against elite competition, gaining a much needed experience boost before high school. By freshman year of high school, any child who played all-stars and travel ball is at such a massive advantage that most of the other kids simply do not make the team and fade away. The experience in Little League All-Star selection often gives such a sour taste to young players that not being selected to the All-Star team is often the last straw in their baseball career. Thankfully for Iceman, he played high school ball and even won a City Championship, but Frenchie ended up quitting baseball and went down a path that put his future in doubt.

To say that Frenchie could have gone down a different path with a more supportive system in place is an understatement. He had all the tools to become an elite baseball player at any level, but his troubled youth coupled with the inequities of his time in Little League caused him to focus on things other than baseball like drugs and alcohol. Sports are more than just a game or a diversion as people often say. Sports can be a ticket out of the cycle of poverty that plagues many families in America. Sports can be the only thing that motivates a kid to maintain grades and keep showing up at school, and if they're taken away from an at-risk kid, that can have a devastating effect on their future. Frenchie was not the first kid I have seen take a bad turn after something went south with a sport that he played, and he certainly won't be the last.

One can only imagine what the baseball careers of Frenchie and Iceman would have been like if not for the biases they faced growing up. Had Iceman not been a forgotten child growing up in the league, he may have been the kind of player who gets drafted. He did not have the opportunities that JP (the league president's son) had, but he nevertheless excelled beyond anything JP could have ever become. Imagine if Iceman had been given the 30 additional games of all-star play, the practices with all-star teammates, the opportunities to play travel ball, etc., that JP had—he could have been a truly special player. He was really good despite all of those obstacles, but it makes you wonder how many thousands of kids just like Iceman suffered similar fates in their Little League careers.

Iceman and Frenchie are just two examples from one season in one league. Imagine if you go through the whole country and look for more. For every story that is told, there are many more that go untold. How many kids simply give in when told, "You're not an all-star," instead of fighting it like Frenchie did? How many kids quit when they face the disappointment of being denied the shot instead of laughing it off and going on to star at the next level like Iceman? All sports are tough, but the exclusionary nature of baseball these days has been far more effective in keeping kids out because baseball requires a lot of repetition and experience to improve. Baseball isn't like football, where a kid can gain 50 pounds as a 15-year-old and suddenly become a top prospect. Baseball isn't like basketball, where a kid can have a growth spurt and suddenly be bombarded with scholarship offers. Baseball isn't like sales, where anyone with the right personality and attitude can be successful. Baseball is more like being a doctor, where you have to go through years of training and seasoning to even be minimally qualified, and generally once you hit a certain age, it's too late to start trying.

Iceman and Frenchie weren't the only kids I coached who were snubbed from getting recognition over the years, but one thing nearly all of those kids have had in common is the fact that they were not White. If a poll was taken across the country of all Little League programs, I can guarantee that the majority of

Black and Brown kids who play in mostly White leagues would tell you that they did not receive a fair shake. They would likely confirm all the inferences I have made throughout this book about positional bias and about bias in all-star selection. Again, many of these issues do not stem from outright hate and racism, but from unconscious biases that everyone has. As a coach, I often reflect on my seasons so that I can understand and learn from my misconceptions and other biases that were turned upside down over the course of the year. Some kids live up to the expectations (whether good or bad), but some kids shock you with wild changes in their personalities or in the revelation of their true selves.

Baseball's problems with race and discrimination are not really the fault of the Major League Baseball organizations and their operations, nor are they the fault of Little League. Baseball's problems really lie in the youth ranks on a micro level. Power hungry Little League parents swoop in and manipulate the system to ensure that their children are given every opportunity, even if those opportunities take chances away from more deserving kids. This results in a vacuum, where kids get discouraged by the game of baseball and shift their focus elsewhere, either to other sports or other activities. Until the types of problems that Iceman and Frenchie faced are a thing of the past, we will continue to see Black and Brown kids opt to play other sports that are more welcoming to them than the game of baseball.

VIDA BLUE

Vida Blue grew up in rural Louisiana in the era of legalized segregation. Vida told me that because he grew up in an all-segregated environment, it meant that he was not really directly exposed to racism as a child. He went to all-Black churches and all-Black schools, and his parents were buried in an all-Black cemetery. His father would say, "Listen, son, you don't wanna be nowhere where you're not wanted[xlix]" whenever Vida wondered why they were not welcomed in certain places. As a result, he was raised to brush aside the issues faced during segregation as minor inconveniences rather than something he should fight against. "We didn't really know what prejudice was because we were generally kept away from it". "It didn't bother me that my parents didn't want to go to the city pools", Vida said, "I didn't know I was missing out on anything because it just wasn't a part of our lives."

Vida's upbringing was modest; In order to earn the money to pay for his first baseball glove, he picked cotton for a week for a man named Horace Dinkins back home in Louisiana. Vida was a talented athlete who excelled in nearly every sport. Eventually, he was a high school football star and one of the most dominant pitchers in the state as a teenager and signed a contract with the Oakland A's to become a professional pitcher. So when Vida was plucked from rural Louisiana and moved to a mostly White community in Burlington, Iowa, he was a stranger in a strange land. Blue was fast-tracked through the Minor Leagues, playing only the 1968 and part of the 1969 season before making his Major League debut. Blue was dominant in the Minors and was largely spared the brunt of the racism that was impacting the majority of Black players at the time. "In Class-A ball, I was like a deer in the headlights. I was just trying to establish myself back then[1]." He was supporting his family back home after his father had passed on, so Vida had a lot of pressure to succeed and to stay away from controversy. "I went there to play baseball, that was my focus, and luckily I survived Burlington, Iowa".

The next year he went to Birmingham, Alabama...in the late 1960s when tensions were extremely high. Vida did not suffer the same level of discrimination and racism as many of his peers, and his theory as to why was rather interesting: "I heard stories of my teammates who played in the outfield who were getting all the racial slurs and stuff being thrown at them. Being a pitcher, I don't remember hearing anything, but I think it was because the people behind home plate paid more for their seats and were generally a higher class of people." Vida was hurt by these revelations from his teammates and truly felt it in his soul. "Why can't you accept me? We're all the same in the eyes of the lord." Vida spoke at length about the power of the spoken and written word to hurt and to cause deep wounds. "Words do hurt, and they go deep".

At the time Vida was making his progress to the Majors, he was seeing stars like Muhammad Ali, Kareem Abdul-Jabbar, and Jim Brown speaking out (often with personal or professional consequences), but most of his fellow Black ballplayers remained silent. "It's not that they didn't have a platform, it's just that they didn't use it. Elgin Baylor, Wilt, you think of all these Black stars in the 70s, but they didn't use their voices then. But now is the time for us to make the changes and make them happen." Vida's passion for the movement's progress in 2020 was evident. Vida has been extremely involved in philanthropic activities for years but has generally been a more quiet activist for change. Speaking about the Black Lives Matter Movement and the NBA walkout in August of 2020, Vida was very candid in his views: "I'm LeBron James, but I'm still a Black man in America. I'm World Champ, but when it comes to being pulled over, I'm still nothing more than a description. I've had 'the talk'".

"The Talk" has two different meanings in America. For White kids, "The Talk" happens when a kid is hitting puberty and their parents sit them down and talk about sex, sexuality, and relationships. A simple Google search of "the talk with your kids" brings you to a bunch of pages talking about the "birds and the bees", but if you add in the simple word of "Black" in front of kids, the result is VERY different. The first result on Google (on September 2, 2020) was the following article: "Having 'The Talk': How Families Prepare Black Children for Police Interactions". In the article, it tells how just about every teenager gets copious safe-driving tips from their parents when they get their first driver's license. But for Black teens, the freedom and independence that comes with driving necessitates an added conversation—one often referred to simply as "the talk." This one offers advice for safely navigating potential encounters with police[li].

The fact that this is such a starkly different moment in a child's life, depending on the color of their skin, is sad, but it also reveals how deep this issue goes in American society. Vida's feeling on this disparity is that it is not causing deliberate ignorance of the problem, but rather it is merely just another piece of the privilege pie. "When you're so privileged, you have a blind eye to the rest of the world." People would ask him why he was mad, and his answer was, "Why you mad? I'm mad because I get fucked with every time I step out of the door...give me something besides 'probable cause'." Vida is extremely focused on changing the world today. He has deep involvement in so many charitable organizations and he feels a strong affinity towards the new generation of ballplayers. "This is not about me, this is about us. I'm just so glad these young players have stepped up to the plate [he did ask me to pardon the pun in this instance] in this moment."

For many athletes, the path to success was extremely precarious and history is littered with extremely talented athletes who had promising careers derailed by one moment in time or a lack of structure keeping them focused on their sport. As a coach, I have seen quite a few of these players over the years, but it has always been much harder for the poor kids to overcome those obstacles, and for those poor kids, the obstacles are often far more numerous than their wealthy peers. While Vida made it, there were countless others like him in the South in the 1960s who suffered from a lack of opportunity, or worse, suffered from the consequences of their situation in life. Those complications could be physical, mental, or psychological, or they could be things like incarceration, lack of opportunity to play, alcoholism or drug abuse, etc. For Vida, baseball was his way out. "Baseball saved my life. During my teenage years I would've been rebelling but instead I was in these small towns playing ball and being held to a higher standard".

In 1971, Vida made history for being the first Black man to start on the hill in an All-Star game. It took 24 years from the time Jackie Robinson integrated baseball to have a Black starting pitcher in the All-Star Game. Interestingly enough, it was the only Major League All-Star game to ever feature two Black starting pitchers. Dock Ellis and Vida Blue started for the National League and American League, respectively, because they were both having historically good seasons. But historically good seasons were never a guarantee for an All-Star start, as Bob Gibson in 1968 would attest to. Because of that history, Dock Ellis made a concerted effort to place pressure on the manager of the National League team, Sparky Anderson. "Ain't no way they gonna start two brothers against each other in the All-Star Game…when it comes to Black players, baseball is backwards and everyone knows it.[lii]" Ellis is a legend in baseball for reasons beyond his all-star performance in 1971 and his politics, but Ellis was also known in baseball circles for his incredible intelligence. By speaking out on the issue, Ellis knew what he was doing—namely, he was setting the stage for people to question why he was *not* the starter if Anderson chose to go in a different direction.

So when Vida and Dock were named as the starting pitchers, it was a shock to many baseball fans and insiders. And, in the 73 years of integrated Major League Baseball between 1947 and 2020, that remains the only time two Black men started opposite each other in the midseason classic. While Ellis was more of a revolutionary, Blue was more of a quiet representative of progress. "I don't know what [that game] did for baseball, but it gave the Black community a chance to be proud of having two Black pitchers start an All-Star Game," Blue said. "It's hard for me to believe that guys like Bob Gibson, Fergie Jenkins, and Don Newcombe never started before me.... I was just happy to be named to the All-Star team," he said. "This was the age of great pitchers like Catfish Hunter and Jim Palmer. ... I walked into the All-Star clubhouse like a kid in a candy store, seeing all of those stars I grew up reading about[liii]." This attitude continues to be how Blue looks at the world.

During our conversation, Vida and I began to speak about how the owners are different in 2020 than in 1972. "The whole league and the owners are getting on board with the movement. What do we do after this? What's next?" The hope that Vida has for the future is apparent. As our conversation moved on to politics, we began to speak about the presidential race between Joe Biden and Donald Trump. Vida is dedicated to helping to get young people involved. "The vote carries the loudest voice," he said. Voting is an important issue for Vida, especially since he grew up in the segregated South during a period in which Black voices were silenced through various voter suppression efforts.

When talking about the rise of the Black Lives Matter movement, Blue spoke with reverence for those who made things happen, while simultaneously expressing a general hesitation for getting directly involved. "This goes beyond me playing a game on the court or being a star on the field. This is bigger than sports, this is bigger than all of us. I'm not a threat to take nobody's job. I don't want nobody else's job but mine. I'm only qualified to throw a baseball." This mentality means that while Blue is deeply committed to the movement, he generally defers to those with a less laid-back nature to take the lead. Blue saw himself as different from some of the more vocal stars at the time like Jim Brown and Muhammad Ali. While he clearly understood his value as a ballplayer, his ego never inflated to the point one would expect of someone who won the AL MVP and Cy Young Award at the age of 22. "I'm not sure why we didn't speak out; maybe it was a different world," he continued. "It wasn't really anyone but the big stars like Ali, Jabbar, Jim Brown, et cetera." I don't really think he realized that HE was one of those big stars, too; after all, he was the best player in the American League in 1971 and one of the best lefthanded pitchers in the history of the game.

Despite being one of the best players in the entire league, Vida too struggled with his career path and with money during his time as a professional baseball player. Before Curt Flood sacrificed his career to help usher in the free agency era, there was a work stoppage in 1972. Blue, despite being the defending AL Most Valuable Player and Cy Young Award winner (awarded to the league's best pitcher), became a plumber. On March 27, 1972, Vida was on the cover of the magazine Sports Illustrated with the headline "Vida Blue, Plumbing Executive". He was trying to get a raise from his low salary, but Oakland owner Charlie Finley only offered him about 60% of what he was asking for. Eventually Blue signed with the team, but he had a terrible season in 1972, going from 24 wins to just 6, and he saw his career fade a bit to a level that made him a member of the "Hall of Very Good," without ever rising to the level of "Surefire Hall-of-Famer" he appeared to be before the holdout. Blue did not suffer the same fate as Curt Flood, but he suffered nonetheless.

After his spectacular 1971 season, Blue demanded a pay raise. In 1971 he had made $14,750 in salary and $6,365.58 as his share of the postseason money. He also got a Cadillac as a bonus from Finley. Finley offered a raise, but not nearly what Blue wanted. Bob Gerst, an attorney representing Blue, presented an opening offer to Finley of $115,000. Later he told Finley that Blue would accept $85,000, which was a little less than the average salary paid to the top ten highest paid pitchers in baseball. Finley said he would pay Blue no more than $50,000. Finley held firm, making the negotiations public and declaring that Blue would not be seeking so much if he had not hired a lawyer to represent him. Both sides made their case to the press and the public, and the acrimonious situation became referred to as "The Holdout."

The situation also served to elevate scrutiny of the reserve clause, which was under new attack by the players. Marvin Miller, director of the Players Association, was critical of Finley and the reserve system. The holdout extended into spring training. On March 16, Blue and Gerst held a televised press conference to announce that Blue was withdrawing from baseball to take a position with the Dura Steel Products Company. While Blue actually did work for the company for a time, this was an effort to combat Finley, because Blue's real desire was to play baseball.

They finally agreed on $63,000, but Finley and Blue couldn't agree on the wording of the announcement of the agreement. Finley did not want to appear as conceding anything, and insisted that he was paying Blue $50,000, an additional $5,000 signing bonus, plus $8,000 for Blue's college fund. Blue wanted the deal to state what it was: payment of $63,000. This was the kind of game that Finley often played with his employees. Finally, on May 2, Blue signed for the package[liv].

Blue's fight for more money may have contributed to the dismantling of the Oakland A's over the next few years, and anyone who has pitched before knows that no matter how good you are on the hill, it is impossible to have extended success in an elite league without a strong team around you. Balls that would have been outs become hits, and as a result, more players reach base, and more of them score. This is evidenced strongly by the statistics, with Blue's BABIP (batting average, balls in play) stat jumping well above his career level. The Oakland A's went from committing 0.89 errors per game to 1.18 errors per game. That 32% increase in the errors committed by Blue's defense meant that every start he was suffering lost outs and downgrades were present at many positions. First base saw a major drop in performance with a nearly 75% increase in the errors committed at that spot. Third base went from high quality defense by Sal Bando to the worst defensive hot corner in the league by a wide margin. Shortstop was another spot with a major drop in defensive performance. For Vida, a pitcher who tended to trend towards being a flyball pitcher, having a weak outfield was especially damaging. Left field saw the number of errors triple from 1976 to 1977, with a simultaneous drop in the number of assists. This major shift in the defensive abilities of the Athletics was a direct cause of Blue's struggles in 1977.

Blue's play suffered because of these changes to the roster and he was no longer one of the best pitchers in baseball just a few years removed from one of the best pitching years in baseball history. Part of the problem was personal, sure, but much of Blue's decline could be blamed on the fire sale that took place in Oakland from 1976 to 1977. Eventually, he was sold to the San Francisco Giants in 1978 and enjoyed a comeback year thanks to the superior defense of the Giants, but that was basically the beginning of the end for Blue as an elite MLB pitcher. In 1983, Blue (now with the Kansas City Royals) struggled mightily. After seven starts and a record of 0-3, he was relegated to the bullpen. He stayed in the pen and made spot starts, but did not pitch well in either role. With a record of 0-5 and an ERA of 6.01, he was released by the Royals on the fifth of August.

Even though his struggles on the field were immense in his later career, Blue's baseball problems paled in comparison with his problems off the field. Blue and Royals teammates Willie Wilson, Jerry Martin, and Willie Mays Aikens were implicated in buying cocaine. Blue pleaded guilty to cocaine possession and served 81 days in prison. On December 15, 1983, he was suspended for a year by Commissioner Kuhn[lv]. When Blue retired he suggested he still struggled with drug addiction by stating "I reached the point where I had to choose between baseball and life.... Along with all the glory that I'd achieved, there was a growing darkness reaching for me. And the light began to dim as early as 1972." This revelation begs the question, "How great would Vida Blue have been without that darkness?" While Vida's story is not necessarily a story of exclusion, it still shows that even when a person is able to achieve so much that there are still so many ways for all of it to come crashing down. Blue is not a cautionary tale, though, because he has enjoyed a wonderful post-playing career as an ambassador for the game and a philanthropist.

TRAVEL BALL & LITTLE LEAGUE

People often ask me the big question: WHY? Why has baseball become such a niche sport after so many years as the national pastime? In my opinion, the biggest reason for this is the proliferation of travel ball and the men who run travel ball programs and "skills" camps or "scouting" camps. This is not the exclusive domain of baseball, but in baseball it is far more impactful, because baseball is a sport that truly requires elite competition to succeed, and travel ball has made it impossible for many kids to remain competitive in the sport. Back in the 1980s and early 1990s, travel ball was in its infancy. It existed, but it was rare and most kids were driven by the motivation that they would one day play for the local high school before moving onto the minor leagues or NCAA ball. During my high school days, travel ball was shut down during the season except for the players who could not play for their school team for one reason or another, and those leagues were extremely weak. I played in the San Mateo Colt league one year and it was a lower quality of baseball than any league I ever played in.

But something happened in the 1990s and younger players started flocking to travel ball programs and away from Little League and Pony League. Baseball is still popular and many kids still play, but Little League is suffering while travel ball programs thrive[lvi]. In Warner Robbins, Georgia, the impact of the rise of travel ball is particularly apparent. The Warner Robbins Little League is one of the most successful programs in the world, but it went from 1000+ kids signed up every year to 524 in 2019. Other leagues saw their numbers drop in similar ways (1500+ to less than 1000), yet the participation numbers for baseball remain steady and may even be on the rise.[lvii] As a result, the opportunities for kids to play against quality competition cheaply via Little League are dropping sharply. Little League used to have all the area's ballplayers during the spring season, and the best kids might play in the summer or fall, but they still all played in that one league. Once travel ball started to become more popular, however, many of those elite players left the Little League world and the quality of play suffered. Back in the 1980s, you could be pretty sure that most of the best players in Little League were the best players in the country for their age group, but these days that really is not the case anymore. Players today who are truly elite will not waste their time playing Little League baseball, opting instead for elite travel teams and the showcase circuit.

Travel ball is big business and the men who run it profit enormously from the game. (I say "men" in this context because sexism plays a major role in baseball's exclusivity. Moreover, I have met only one female travel ball coach in my lifetime—she was also the only female umpire in my league.) If a kid wants to excel in baseball these days, they will be told every step of the way that they NEED to play travel ball. This is not free to do, so kids who are not immediately serious about baseball may get left behind. A kid may like baseball enough to play 20 games in the Spring as an 8 year old, but not enough to commit to the sport at that age. Five years later that kid may suddenly realize they want to play baseball at a higher level and they realize that the only way to do that is to play travel ball, with teams where the players are likely to be far more advanced than them due to their travel ball experience. Unfortunately, the costs to play travel ball are astronomical[lviii] and when compared to Little League, the difference is staggering. For a child to play both Spring and Fall ball with a local Little League, it will cost between $140 and $200, depending on the league. For a child to get the same number of games with a travel program will cost at least 10 times that, if not more, and this essentially prices all children from lower income backgrounds out of the game. A season of Little League for $75 is actually a great deal, but for many kids that $75 is the difference between their family being able to make the rent that month or not, so adding another $500–1000 for lower tier travel ball is a nonstarter for most low income families.

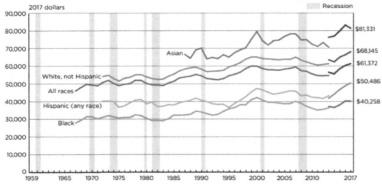

Real Median Household Income by Race and Hispanic Origin: 1967 to 2017

Figure 6

The graphs in Figure 6 show that the racial demographics

of baseball are impacted significantly by the income level of

each demographic group. Notice how the racial disparity in

youth baseball seems to impact the Hispanic and Black players

more than White and Asian players. A Black family makes

$40,000 on average, meaning they are unlikely to be able to

spend $3000 for their child to play baseball, when AAU

basketball is significantly cheaper and requires far less

commitment to gain recognition for college scholarships. For

example, a kid can have one good game at a basketball showcase and burst onto the national scene as a major prospect, but with baseball it takes a lot longer to establish yourself as a prospect. The ROI (return on investment) for a 10 year old athlete whose parents are choosing between baseball and basketball due to costs are always going to favor basketball. Add in the fact that a top-of-the-line basketball costs no more than $85 (the most expensive basketball at Dick's Sporting Goods' website on 7/10/2020 was $84.95) and no glove less than $150 is even worth buying, and it starts to become clearer. Why sign your child up for baseball when they're going to need hundreds of dollars in equipment every year, in addition to the league fees, when a basketball lasts many years and the only other equipment needed are shoes, which can be transitioned to daily attire once broken down too much for competitive play, unlike baseball cleats.

This in turn hurts the game in the long-run because more than almost any other sport, baseball is patrilineal. Young boys often learn baseball from their fathers through games of catch or trips to the ballgame (few places are more likely to see a father and son spending time together than a ballpark on a Saturday afternoon) and this is another factor in the death of the game in the inner-city. I will delve into the "fatherless" aspect of the debate, because many studies have shown that Black fathers are actually MORE involved with their children than their White counterparts[lix], so the main factor in this patrilineal nature of baseball is the fact that Black fathers simply do not see baseball as a place for their child. Suppose a young low-income Black child grows up to be wealthy as an adult, will he be more likely to enroll his child in a sport where he was excluded as a child or one where he was welcomed with open arms? A Black man who grew up excluded from baseball is not likely to buy a glove for his son and have a catch. And, because most kids grow up in relatively segregated neighborhoods and schools[lx], they are not likely to feel any peer influence towards the game of baseball.

Another major barrier for baseball is the fact that it is a very skill-based sport. Kids struggle to come to the game at more advanced ages than other sports because of the high level of skill needed. As a coach in extremely low income neighborhoods, I have seen this firsthand. A team full of kids who have never played before has absolutely no chance against a team full of travel ball kids. Scores like 38-0 and 31-0 (in just 2.5 innings) happen because the gap in skill simply cannot be compensated for with any level of physical athletic talent. A team full of players from a football team that was competitive at the statewide level and a state championship basketball program could succeed in track and field, but in baseball that team goes 0-16 at the second lowest division in the state[lxi]. This leads to a faucet effect (wherein the water goes into the sink from the faucet only to quickly vanish down the drain), where players try out baseball for a year or two and grow tired of the losing and growing pains and then go onto running track in the spring because athletic talent alone can carry them a lot further. This is not to say that track does not require skill to be elite—it does. And it takes a ton of hard work to be great in track and field, but I have seen countless young athletes join the track team and come in the top three in a meet within a week. Baseball players do not often bat .400 or dominate on the mound with no experience.

This is not to say that young Black kids cannot become skilled, but rather that they are kept from even trying the game because by the time they can convince their parents to sign them up for baseball they have already fallen far behind the kids who have been playing since age 4. Without a childhood spent playing T-Ball, most kids from low income neighborhoods simply cannot join in the fun later on.

Baseball is a scary sport for a lot of kids, too. During one of my practices, several of my players who also play football were struggling with fielding ground balls. They were flinching and not getting directly in front of the ball, so I asked them, "Which is scarier, fielding a grounder or being hit by a linebacker?" Without a moment of hesitation, they all replied in unison: "Grounders!" Thus, the fear factor is one of the most significant barriers kids face when trying baseball. Nearly every season I have at least one new player who takes a ball to the face and then never gets back on the field. This fear decreases as skill and experience increase, but it is extremely hard for kids to gain that skill and experience if they're too scared to even play the game.

Another issue is that kids see home runs and big breaking curveballs and think they can do the same, but they simply cannot, because even experienced players struggle to achieve those things. I was a home run hitter at times in my career, but I also went extended periods without hitting any balls over the fence. In my six years coaching high school ball, I have never had a player hit a home run over the fence. Throwing a curveball is hard, too. Sure, I have had players pick up a decent curveball in a single bullpen session, but many pitchers spend years trying to perfect the curve with absolutely no success. Kids want instant gratification, and taking batting practice during their first time on a baseball field usually results in an embarrassing mix of dinky grounders and swing-and-misses. This initial failure does not come with a cherry on top. The cherry for a kid starting baseball doesn't come until they have dedicated many hours to their craft. And even then, they may never have the power to hit a home run. Even a person with absolutely no skill or athleticism can shoot a basketball and get lucky enough to put it in the basket. A prime example of this would be my good friend Danny D'Ull, who used to come to my basketball practices after school and launch shots from half court and could sink them at a pretty good rate. Danny was NOT even a remotely decent basketball player, but he could make that shot.

Another major challenge with getting kids into baseball at a later age is that it is a sport where failure is commonplace and where opportunities to succeed come at random intervals and always have outside factors involved. It is a sport that is unforgiving to those without skill because it is unforgiving to those WITH skill, too. Even in the Major Leagues, players fail regularly. More than a half dozen players committed 20 errors in the field and 157 players struck out 100 or more times in 2019.

A sport where the best of the best fail so frequently has an extremely high barrier to entry, even for people with all the financial resources and physical tools in the world. Baseball has also become a more difficult sport since the explosion of travel ball and single sport specialization. According to FanGraphs, the average fastball in 2002 was 89.9 miles per hour and by 2013, it was 91.7[lxii]. With less than a half a second to react to a MLB level fastball, many players strike out quite frequently.

Most people never become Major League baseball players, but at the Little League level the difference between the good and the not-so-good is even more staggering. Every year during the Little League World Series, there are kids throwing 70+ MPH, and at 46 feet away compared to 60.5 feet in the Major Leagues, that is equivalent to the reaction time for a 90 MPH fastball. Most kids throw 50–60 MPH at that age level, but every league has a couple of kids who can throw 65, 70, or even 75 MPH, and those are the kids who often intimidate a lot of the less developed young players. Talent/skill gaps are often more significant at younger ages before the weaker players are weeded out, so many kids never make it to the Little League Division (11–13 years old) because they have already been convinced that baseball is not for them. Little League has a wonderful mission. The goal is to get kids involved in a team sport to teach them about life through the medium of baseball. Winning is not supposed to be a goal of regular season games, only the all-star tournament. However, this is simply not how it works in practice. Many Little League coaches at ANY age have one goal, and that is to win. It doesn't matter if the kids are 7 years old or 14, the best player will be at shortstop or pitcher and bat in the top 4 of the lineup and play the entire game, while the worst player will play their required minimum time (6 defensive outs and 1 at-bat) and then ride the bench the rest of the game.

My first year coaching Little League Juniors (13–14 year old kids) I had this incredible player named Joey. He was easily one of the most talented kids in the country at his age with a high-70s fastball with a lot of movement, a sharp curveball, and a ton of power as a hitter. Early in the season, we were winning a game pretty handily and I benched him in the 4th inning so a different kid could get a chance to play the entire game. Several minutes after making the move, I noticed him in the corner of the dugout looking dejected. I asked him why he was so upset, because we were winning and he had played a good game, and his response was, "I've never sat on the bench before". He had played for 9 years and never once sat out a defensive inning. This was not his fault—it was the fault of his coaches over the years. Joey struggled when he got older because he had never been taught how to watch others succeed—he was always the star. For kids like that, high school ball can be devastating to their ego. Freshmen in Southern California rarely star on a varsity team, and you often see youth stars quit at this point, too.

The real problem is not that he always got to play, but rather that for those ~180 games, he got about 1000 innings in the field while Julian (who started a few years later but had always been the last man on the roster type) would have had only about 400 innings in the field. So, not only did they have a gap in talent and skill, they also had a severe experience gap that widened the gap between them as baseball players even further. Thankfully for Julian, he was an extremely dedicated player who became an All-Star with my team because he stayed an hour after every practice to work on his bunting skills, his defense, and his pitching. He eventually got to play high school ball, but his story is an exception. Most kids who are like Julian growing up in Little League end up quitting after age 11[lxiii] for a combination of financial reasons and the skill gaps becoming more significant. And again, this is even more significant because the better players generally play travel ball and get better faster than the kids who don't. So, not only are they missing out on time in the field during their recreational season (because Little League is not supposed to be competitive until the tournament play), but they also miss out in the offseason and off days. As a result, you have some kids playing 350+ innings a year, while other kids are getting 350 innings over the course of 7+ years, because they can't afford travel ball and their Little League coaches only play them for the required minimum.

MEXICAN LEAGUE

Mexico's baseball league was a place where Black players could play side-by-side with White players before they could in America. First Jackie Robinson and then Larry Doby integrated the Major Leagues in 1947, but from 1937 to 1946, there were more than 150 US-born Black players in Mexico playing professional ball in a league which was arguably as strong as the MLB at the time[lxiv]. Fourteen of those players have been elected to the Hall of Fame, including Satchel Paige and Josh Gibson, who are among the greatest baseball players of the pre-integration era. Monte Irvin, another one of the Black stars to appear in Mexico, said "It was the first time in my life that I felt free. We could go anywhere we wanted, eat anywhere we wanted, do anything we wanted and not have to worry about anything." This was in stark contrast to the experiences of players like Wilmer Aaron and Terry Whitfield in the United States decades later.

The man who made this all possible was Jorge Pasquel, who according to Monte Irvin, was the George Steinbrenner of Mexico. He was the owner of the biggest import-export business in the country. Rich, handsome, and fierce, Pasquel knew no limits. His larger-than-life persona included dating Maria Felix, Mexico's biggest movie star at the time. He brought glamour to the baseball diamond at the same time that he angled for popularity as a politician. Officially, Jorge Pasquel entered the Mexican Baseball League in 1940 as the owner of a new team, the Azules de Veracruz. But before that, he was the main sponsor of the league, signing and paying Black stars to play for all the league's teams[lxv].

With his connections and wallet, Pasquel recommended a Black Cuban superstar named Martin Dihigo to the Aguila baseball club, also in Veracruz in 1937. Martin Dihigo carried the team to the championship in 1937 and 1938. The Mexico City Agrario team, archrival to the Aguila club, countered by signing Satchel Paige. Paige was the greatest Black American pitcher of the time, and in 1938 became the first American-born Black player to officially appear in the Mexican League. By 1940, there were 63 African-American players in Mexico—a Mexican "Field of Dreams." Pasquel built it, and they came. His master plan was to have Major League caliber baseball in Mexico during the summer season. To do this, he strengthened his relationship with the Cuban League, which played in the winter, to guarantee that his stars could work all year long[lxvi].

The 1940s in Mexico saw stars like Martin Dihigo, Cool Papa Bell, Josh Gibson, Ray Dandridge, Wild Bill Wright, and Willie Wells playing in the Mexican league, when in America they would have been relegated to a segregated league. Players were able to excel in Mexico because they were treated like human beings and not like second class citizens. Most teams had several Black players, too, so each Black player in Mexico was not just a token for his team. Instead, he was just one of the guys and it was clearly not an issue for any one of their teammates. This was such a stark difference from what was happening in the

United States at the time that many Black players followed the stars down south and enjoyed great success without all the pitfalls of playing in leagues that did not want them there.

Willie Wells was another player who enjoyed being in Mexico. "We live in the best hotels, we eat in the best restaurants. We don't enjoy such privileges in the U.S. I didn't quit Newark and join some other team in the United States. I quit and left the country. I've found freedom and democracy here, something I never found in the United States. Here, in Mexico, I am a man." This mentality was something that many Black people in America can relate to. At some point, the hopelessness of subjugation and secondary status wears on a person, and the best option for change is often a change of scenery. While it may seem difficult to comprehend the feelings that would lead someone to give up on their own country, the experience of Willie Wells can give a valuable bit of evidence to better empathize with the players who made the decision to move down south to Mexico.

It was not just the Black players who made the choice to relocate to Mexico, many White players found the grass greener on the other side of the Rio Grande, too. White American players like Danny Gardella, Sal Maglie, Lou Klein, Max Lanier, Mickey Owen, Vernon Stephens, and others, took the offer and left the Major Leagues, ignoring their contracts and going south as well. White Latino players like Roberto Ortiz, Luis Rodríguez Olmo, Adrián Zabala, Salvador Hernández, Tomás de la Cruz, and several others did the same. Jorge Pasquel had essentially declared war on the U.S. Major Leagues. He offered blank contracts to superstars such as Ted Williams, Bob Feller, and Joe DiMaggio so the players could name their price. They ultimately refused to jump to Mexico, but Pasquel had shown his hand. His bold move could have caused a seismic shift in the game of baseball had any of those megastars accepted his offer, but it winds up in the bin of "what if" moments in history instead.

Mexico offered solace to many Black players because the off-field challenges faced in America could really wear on a man. As Terry Whitfield told me, it made a huge impact being able to find a decent place to stay, and housing discrimination was just not a thing that Black players in Mexico had to worry about. People simply do not understand what it is like to deal with the daily burden of racism unless they have personally faced it. It is not simply an inconvenience that you can just get over, because it is deeper than just dealing with jerks. Black players in the US would have to stay across town from the ballpark while their White teammates could stay across the street. Black ballplayers would have far fewer decent accommodations available to them and their play and development as a player could suffer greatly as a result. This in turn gave White players a distinct advantage over Black players at every level of baseball in America.

Mexico did not take off as an alternate destination for elite baseball players like it should have, but it gave some players a place where they could hone their craft. Many players were given opportunities in Mexico, but many more missed out on those chances. Some of the best players of the Negro Leagues at some point left their baseball cleats printed in Mexico's history. A total of 205 players who left the United States to play south of the border were identified by The Center for Negro League Baseball Research. Players like Josh Gibson, Ray Danbridge, Roy Campanella, and Monte Irvin were all honored in Mexico's Hall of Fame. Bob Kendrick, President of the Negro League Baseball Museum, believes that Jorge Pasquel's recruiting of Black players was instrumental in applying pressure on the MLB to integrate[lxvii]. This pressure from the actions of Jorge Pasquel may never be quantified, but they simply cannot be overlooked.

WOMEN IN BASEBALL

"YOU PLAY BALL LIKE A GIRL!!!" I know pretty much anyone who has a passing interest in the game of baseball has heard this line from the movie "The Sandlot". If taken at face value, it implies that girls are inferior baseball players to boys, but if you look at it a bit deeper, it implies that girls do not belong on the same field as boys. At the high school level, boys and girls are separated into two different sports that are basically the same but with slightly different rules. Why do they really need to be gendered sports? Why can't fastpitch softball and baseball just both be coed sports? Why are girls constantly pressured into switching from baseball to softball? What difference is there between the two sports, really?

Once when I was coaching baseball practice, I was using a pre-chalked field from about 5:00–7:00 in the evening, and at about 6:45 a very large man came up to me and he was quite upset. He told me that they had the field at 7:00 PM for a game between two nationally ranked men's fastpitch softball teams and I had ruined their lines and the dirt in the field with my team. To make it up to him, I agreed to play on his team that night because one of their players had called in and said he couldn't make it. I came to the plate twice, and while I did put the ball in play, both were grounders to third (I NEVER hit the ball the opposite way—I've been a dead-pull hitting lefty my whole life) because it was so hard to catch up to the fastball being thrown from so close. I didn't even get out of the box on the first one because the ball was hit hard and the defensive play was made quickly. It was an eye-opening moment for me.

My experience playing fastpitch after a lifetime of thinking it was "just for girls" proved to me that the sport was simply a different kind of baseball. In a way, it is not really even the same sport because different techniques and tactics are necessary for success. A different kind of swing is needed. Pitchers use a different kind of throwing motion and the field is a different size. So, it really is a completely different sport and not just an easier version of baseball as people often say.

In reality, there could easily be a fastpitch and a baseball team at a school and they could both be coed sports. Both are easily played by boys or girls, and both require essentially the same equipment, skills, and physical tools. Both sports require high degrees of hand-eye coordination and timing, and both sports have a wide range of speed, strength, and size among its players. Baseball and softball players come in all shapes and sizes and range in speed and strength far more than any other sport. Football has a wide range as well, but the physical nature of football means it is a sport that places a strong emphasis on speed and strength—far more so than baseball and softball.

The idea behind Jim Crow was that Blacks and Whites would be kept segregated with "separate but equal" facilities, even though they were hardly equal. In many ways, the gendered sports of softball and baseball play out like Jim Crow. There are many girls throughout the country who would rather play baseball but are told by coaches, peers, principals, and so on that they can only play softball. Even girls who excel at the

Little League level eventually are pushed into softball, including Mo'ne Davis, the most famous baseball playing girl in recent memory. Davis dominated the boys for a whole summer when she was 12, gaining national stardom and appearing on the covers of countless magazines and newspapers. But Mo'ne did not play baseball in high school or college. She played softball. Why is that?

I met Mo'ne at the after party of the ESPY Awards the year after she had her breakout. I simply told her she was an inspiration to one of my players, a girl who, despite being older than Davis by a couple of years, looked up to her in awe. Martha was that girl's name, and Martha was obsessed with baseball. She not only loved playing the game, she also loved watching it, reading about it, talking about it, and dreamed of one day making a movie about it. Martha was simply a female reflection of myself at that age. Everything in life revolved around baseball. But Martha was a 12-and-a-half year old girl, and girls that age face a ton of pressure from every side. Putting even more pressure on Martha was the fact that she was still into "girly" things like Disney princesses, puppies, and babies. She was the only person on the team who squealed when someone showed up at our field with a cute puppy and was clearly different from her teammates. So, when Martha came into the league offices to sign up for the upcoming season, she reluctantly began to sign up for softball. I started talking to her about her goals in the sport and she kept talking about baseball and not softball.

I looked at her and asked, "Do you want to play baseball or softball?" She meekly told me she wanted to play baseball, but people were telling her to switch to softball because she could not play baseball in high school. As the head of the 13–14 year old division (Juniors), I was in a position to ensure she was placed onto my team and could earn the playing time she deserved. I told her not to let anyone tell her what she can and can't do and that if she wanted to keep playing baseball that she had a place on my team. She decided to stick with baseball and came out to practice with my team. None of the players treated her differently and she worked hard to fit in as a ballplayer, not as a "girl playing baseball". This is a common theme in the "girls playing baseball" movement. The players do not seem to care. If the girl is one of the best nine on their team, they generally do not have any objections to her being in the lineup. The issues usually arise with opponents and with coaches.

Martha did not play that well in her first season with me as her coach, but she worked really hard and became a very strong player for me soon thereafter. She became an excellent hitter and started to force her way into the heart of the lineup with regular doubles to right-center field. Soon, Martha was confident enough to try out for the high school program and she made the JV baseball team, but it was not easy on her. The coach treated her differently and had her doing managerial duties, taking pictures, getting water, and playing a supporting role to the boys on the team. On the JV team she mostly sat on the bench despite having the team's highest on base percentage and serious gap power. I knew she was capable of playing alongside those boys because I had been the coach for many of the boys at that high school and Martha had frequently outplayed them over the years.

Martha eventually made the varsity team, but was still treated like a second-class citizen, often being asked to take care of administrative/managerial tasks rather than being treated like any other ballplayer. She got the opportunity to play in several games and got on base in four of her five plate appearances, an on base percentage of .800. If I had a player who got on base 80% of the time, I would certainly give them more than five plate appearances. Who knows how much she could have produced if she was given a real opportunity to play like her male teammates. Martha still loves the game to this day and for her it is deeper than just a love for a sport: "Many people have asked me 'why baseball?' And my answer again and again was 'because it makes me feel close to my grandpa who lives in Guanajuato.' The game became this bridge of passion for both of us. Even though I didn't see him as often only when I'd visited

Mexico. It always felt he was always there for me at every game and practice. Every visit was filled with stories from when he played baseball. My grandpa would always ask me if I was still playing and take out his old baseballs and show me how he'd throw people down from home plate excitingly." Who was I to tell Martha that her passion for baseball was wrong and that she should give up that connection to her grandfather?

"I didn't tell anyone why I wanted to play because it was quite silly...I'm the only girl in my family and my dad immigrated from Guanajuato and I wanted to get to know people. It was just a way of being connected, especially to my grandpa who played the equivalent of AAA ball in Mexico. It was a form of saying 'I'm honoring your legacy because I want to feel connected to you because I want to, not because I have to.' I could probably get scholarships from softball but that wasn't the goal. My dad also got much more connected to me after I played baseball, and he even became involved in my teams as the 'team dad'. It was more of a way to be connected to the male figures in my family[lxviii]."

For Martha, the struggle was more than just one where she felt like an outsider as a girl playing baseball, she also dealt with physical struggles. Martha is short and not overly athletic, but she did have unique strength and hand-eye coordination for a girl of her stature. But she fell behind her teammates often during conditioning. "During conditioning is when things would fall apart for me because I am not as fast or tall as the guys. I was fit for a woman but not fit or built like a man. Conditioning was really hard. They wouldn't make fun of me, they would just keep silent. 'You are a team, you can't leave anyone behind...but you can leave me?'" She would often work out so hard that she would throw up from the intensity of the workout. She eventually bridged the gap between her and her teammates, but she still struggled to keep up.

For Martha, the silence was deafening at times. "Silence shouldn't be a problem, but sometimes silence hurts more than words. Because it's just you and your inner self struggling. But when you're digging into the ground through your cleats and all you really see is the backs of your teammates, it's really hard. I felt as though I was a burden." Martha was never a burden, but that feeling was real because she dealt with microaggressions every day as a girl playing baseball. When Martha went out for the team her first year, the experience was less than perfect. "The coach at the time said 'I appreciate your fire, but you aren't at our standards and unfortunately you aren't going to make the team.' The coach who had helped me was Latino and it was nice because I rarely ever had any Latino coaches. The head coach was different, though; he was reported to have said, 'I will quit before I have a girl on my team.'" Unfortunately, that sentiment is not uncommon for girls to hear from coaches when they're trying to play baseball.

For Martha, a budding filmmaker who was accepted into USC Film School, creating a legacy was not about going to the Majors and making millions of dollars. Martha knows her time as a baseball player at San Diego High School was a success because several girls there followed her lead and played baseball. She has used her experience as a baseball player to develop as a filmmaker: "The thing about film, the connections you build inside the field are the connections you bring outside the field. You build these lifelong friendships and mentorships that go with me to this day. They are always there for me. They made a family, the team isn't just a team, it's a family. A diverse community. Baseball has prepared me to basically just be, just take it in. It's sad to say that I'm used to it, but I've dealt with so much in my experience that I use it as a way to communicate the issues to the public through my work in film." The lack of real opportunities beyond her limited high school playing experience (and I say limited because she really did not get to play as much as she deserved to) meant that Martha's love for baseball had to be expressed through her work in film and not on the field. Had she been about 20 years older, she may have seen her opportunities differently because of the presence of a special team called the Colorado Silver Bullets.

In the 1990s the Colorado Silver Bullets were a baseball team, sponsored by a beer company, who played against amateur all-star teams and semi-pro teams. What made this baseball team unique, other than the fact that it was a truly independent team gaining national notoriety, was that it was made up of all women. At first they did not enjoy much success, but after a few years they were able to put together a winning record before losing their sponsorship and folding. The team was successful because it showed that women could play baseball and compete with men, but it was a failure, too, because it was simply not profitable enough to continue beyond a couple of years and it never really rose above the level of being a publicity stunt. It did not spawn any leagues for women to play baseball and it did not give rise to all-girls Little League or high school baseball teams. No players were given any real opportunities to play with men, though a couple of players did get publicity-stunt-style appearances at the Minor League level: After the 1994 season, Lee Anne Ketcham and Julie Croteau became the first women to sign with the Class A and AA men's Hawaii Winter Baseball League, and in 1996 Pam Davis, in a guest appearance with the AA Jacksonville Suns, pitched a scoreless inning of relief against the Australian Olympic men's team.

Despite the challenges facing women in the sport, a young girl named Justine Siegal set a goal for herself: To play baseball. As a T-Ball player, Justine was one of four girls on her team, but soon after that it was just her and another girl playing baseball[lxix]. By the time she was 12, she was the only girl left in her peer group still playing baseball. This was not a unique situation for Justine, however, because she was also the only girl on her soccer team. Justine just loved to play sports and never saw herself as any different from her fellow athletes. By age 13, things began to shift for her. That was the age a coach first told her that he did not want her on the team and that she belonged on a softball field. Instead of giving up, Justine used this exclusion as motivation to excel.

"My high school wouldn't let me try out until I played

against them," Justine said proudly. Her competitive spirit apparent in every answer, Justine simply does not believe in the idea that someone cannot do something simply because society says they can't. Justine began to face more and more barriers as she got older, and she began to realize that playing professional (men's) baseball was probably not in the cards, but she still believed she had what it took to become a professional coach. It was at age 16, after repeatedly being denied opportunities to play summer ball, that Justine got the idea of becoming a college coach.

"No man will listen to a woman on a baseball field" was what one coach told her when she informed him of her goal to coach college baseball. This did not deter her, it simply gave her more energy to charge forward. "I was shy, but I was determined. It didn't make sense to me that he could say that all men wouldn't listen, so I decided to find my own path." So Justine did what only an extremely determined person could possibly do: She designed her own college major and then got a

Ph.D. Justine became a college coach while she was at Springfield College getting her Ph.D., but it was actually at a rival school first before she convinced the coach at Springfield to hire her. Her career did not take off immediately and she had to fight and scrap for every opportunity.

In 2009, Ila Borders (the first female pitcher to start a men's NCAA or NAIA college baseball game as well as the first to start a men's professional game) was working with Mike Veeck in the Independent Leagues when Justine reached out and got an opportunity to coach for one of the independent teams. At that point, she began to get chances to throw batting practice for MLB teams and that is when her name became synonymous with the movement for gender equality in coaching. She attended scout school and then the Oakland A's hired her. But being the first woman took a toll on Justine and she had to deal with so much failure and rejection. However, Justine saw herself as a lightning rod for future generations. "My daughter was born when I was 23 and I wanted to make a better future for her."

Justine had many opportunities to give up or break down, but she rose above it all and became a world-changer.

"You're a really nice doll and all, but I can go to a bar and get a doll." Imagine hearing a manager tell you that when you are just trying to be a baseball coach. Justine did. The same man who told her that was eventually won over, though, and even provided Justine with a recommendation for a future coaching role. The thing is, the players never really gave her any grief— it was always ownership and other coaches who did. As a coach, I can say from experience that the baseball coaching community is extremely closed off and not at all welcoming to new blood that does not fit in with the norm (the norm being a middle-aged White guy with a pickup truck, a gut, a gravely voice, and a blue-collar profession outside of the game). Justine faced scrutiny at every level and was not seen as just another coach, but rather as an oddity to be questioned. Despite being a lifelong baseball nut and expert on the game, she was often treated like a publicity stunt. "Pitching was my specialty and I can't remember being asked a single question about pitching." That speaks volumes about the type of respect given to her compared to her male counterparts.

As Justine began to realize that her mission was futile without a path for others to follow her, she created a girl's baseball team and then founded the non-profit "Baseball For All". In 2015, she presided over the first national baseball tournament specifically for young women and the support from Major League Baseball began to increase. Some people questioned why Justine, an advocate for equality, would want to create leagues specifically for girls, but her explanation shines light on the problem. "I love coed sports and I love when girls and boys play together, but there is a lack of access and equal opportunity for girls on coed teams. A girl on a coed team has to fight to get the chance to play, but on a team of all-girls her playing time will be based solely on her abilities. The idea is to grow girl's baseball leagues so that your granddaughter can play just like your grandson."

"What's incredible is that there are still rules in place that exclude girls from boy's programs. In NYC a girl has to pass a fitness test that the boys don't have to take and even then it's still at the discretion of the AD." Justine explained the issue in great depth. "A middle school girl wanted to play and the entire conference said that they would refuse to play against that school if the girl was on the team." This was a perfect example of the barriers that girls face when they just want to play the game with their peers. Estimates show that only 1 in every 3000+ players who set foot on a Little League field ever even make it to the Majors[lxx], so a world where every kid is able to walk onto a baseball field and feel like they belong is a world worth fighting for. Playing Little League is not about being the next Mike Trout. Even the best kids at the Little League World Series are unlikely to ever play professionally, so it should be about community building and playing a fun game.

"If you tell the girls they can't play baseball, what else will they think they can't do? To me, girls playing baseball is a social justice issue. One day it'll just be about baseball. There has never been less resistance." Justine has set forth in motion a lot of things that cannot be reversed. It is only a matter of time before her influence on the game is as recognizable as Curt Flood's was.

Girls in baseball is an important issue because baseball is a sport where physical limitations are not nearly as significant as other major sports. Women and men are built differently and there are significant genetic differences in the size, strength, speed, and other aspects of athleticism for the average man and woman. There are few, if any, women built strongly enough with the skills to play in the NBA, NFL, or NHL, but baseball is a different kind of sport. At age 16, a player named Jose Altuve attended a Houston Astros' tryout camp in Maracay, Venezuela. The team's scouts didn't allow him to participate, however, because they decided he was too short and they suspected that he had lied about his age[lxxi]. The next day, with encouragement from his father, Altuve returned to the camp and produced his birth certificate. Al Pedrique, then a special assistant for the Astros, asked Altuve, "Can you play?" Altuve looked him in the eye and said, "I'll show you." Pedrique championed him to the front office, convincing them that he had the talent and strength to eventually play in the Major Leagues[lxxii]. The club gave him an evaluation, and after he impressed team officials, they signed him to a contract as an undrafted free agent on March 6, 2007, giving him a small ($15,000) bonus.

Altuve is not a woman, but he represents the uniqueness of the game of baseball. Altuve is the shortest player (officially) since Freddie Patek retired in 1981 and someone who does not have the kind of physical tools that scouts seek, but Altuve has become one of the best players in baseball. He had four straight seasons of 200 hits, leading the league each time, and was the league leader in batting average four times and he was the league's Most Valuable Player (MVP) in 2017. He also became a notable power hitter, smacking 24 homers in 2016 and 2017 and 31 homers in 2019.

I am willing to bet that if you had been at that scout camp in Maracay and you had pointed at Altuve and said "In a decade, that guy will be one of the best hitters in baseball and a five-time Silver Slugger," the other scouts would have laughed you off the field. But baseball is a funny sport, where physical tools are only a small fraction of what makes a great player. While it is a bit of a stretch in logic, the story of Jose Altuve shows that women are capable of competing with men in baseball if they are provided the right opportunities. Players like Altuve prove that size, speed, and strength are important, but they do not need to be in such abundance that only a man could possess the levels necessary to play at the top level. Sure, for every Altuve, there are guys like Frank Thomas or Aaron Judge who are 6'5"+ behemoths, but the simple fact that Altuve outhit every single player in the MLB (according to the statistic Offensive Wins Above Replacement) in 2017 shows that someone at 5'6" and 165 pounds could be an elite MLB hitter.

Bailey Vick, on the other hand, was one of the best hitters

in college softball in 2020, when she batted .556 and then decided to take a job in finance[lxxiii]. I bring up Bailey Vick at this time because she could easily have the skills to play baseball at the next level and she is the same exact size as Altuve. She may have been capable of being a minor league baseball player. She did not have much power, but batting .556 at the Division 1 level is not an easy feat. Surely her hand-eye coordination would translate to baseball.

Kate Gordon, another top softball player, may have even more of a claim that she could be an elite hitter in any league. In her college softball career she hit for a .420/.485/.867 slashline (BA/OBP/SLG) and also played strong defense with a .980 career fielding percentage. In her 602 at bats, she had 253 hits, 194 runs scored, 56 doubles, 6 triples, 67 home runs, 194 RBIs, 81 walks, and only 63 strikeouts. I repeat, she had 67 homers and only 63 strikeouts[lxxiv]. Compared to one of the best power hitters in college baseball in her peer group, Nick Gonzales from New Mexico State, Gordon has much better ratios[lxxv]. In college, Gonzales hit 37 home runs while striking out 79 times[lxxvi]. This is not to say that Gordon has more power than Gonzales, but rather that the numbers show that she at least has potential to be in a similar class of ballplayer as him, especially since her fielding percentage and strikeout rates were both significantly better. They are both basically the same size, with Gonzales being only about 2" taller, and have both shown an elite level of talent and commitment to the sport in comparison to their peers. I don't know if Kate Gordon could be a Major League or even Minor League hitter, but if I was a GM, I would take a chance on someone like her with a late-round draft pick or sign her as an undrafted free agent. If she hit .071 and struck out in 80% of her at bats, it would show that she wasn't ready yet, but if she came in and held her own, it could obliterate a ton of barriers.

Why is there not more of a push for women in baseball? The game lends itself to skill over talent and physical tools, so why haven't more girls been pushed into it? Softball plays a major role in this, but in reality, both sports can be coed. Sure, some men have physical advantages over women in athletics, but all-time great softball player Jennie Finch is taller than Hall-of-Famers Pedro Martinez and Craig Biggio, so where do those limitations truly get blurred in baseball? Height and weight matter a ton in football or basketball, and hockey places a growing importance on the mass of its players, but baseball players are judged far more on the specific skills those players have.

Baseball also has much more room for diversity of skills than other sports. If you are an NBA team building around a specific kind of player, each player on the roster has to fit a very specific role. In the NFL, positions dictate height, weight, running times, etc. You simply cannot make the NFL as a 145-pound ANYTHING, but if you can catch up to a 98 MPH fastball, you can pretty much have any body type. Still, that does not change the fact that many players are overlooked for their physical differences. Some teams shied away from pursuing

Devaris "Dee" Gordon because he was 5'11" inches tall and weighed about 150 pounds coming up. They viewed Gordon as a small kid with little power. The long season schedule was cited as a potential problem[lxxvii]. Despite those concerns, Gordon was a league leader in hits in 2015 and even won a Silver Slugger award. Gordon never showed much power, but he was an asset to his team because he could put the ball in play and was incredibly fast.

Another player, Sam Fuld, proved that being a 5'8" player with diabetes could not stop him from carving out a nice eight-year Major League career and eventually the role as General Manager for the Philadelphia Phillies. I knew Sam in high school, where he was the legendary player everyone talked about when I came to Phillips Exeter. I had the same dreams as him and did not have the same physical limitations. I had three or four inches on him and could throw harder, but he was so much better than me because of his dedication and work ethic. While I spent time playing other sports, computer games, watching episodes of *The Simpsons* over and over, and messing around with girls, Sam was working on his craft. He dominated the competition in New England and earned a scholarship to Stanford, where he continued to excel. Eventually he got drafted and fought his way to the Majors despite his physical limitations. Fuld gained fame for his defense and was employed by several teams mainly due to his outstanding defense and his ability to put the ball in play, but he was more proof that size and other limitations matter far less in baseball than other sports.

These players' stories are so important because the league still ignores players like them. Being undersized is still a major red flag and the eyeball test often removes players from the conversation of "who should we draft/sign?". This is far more true when it comes to females in the game of baseball. Martha's story showed that even when a girl has the ability to compete with boys, she faces serious headwinds due to the fact that most baseball coaches do not see female baseball players as being potentially equal to their male counterparts. Justine stated multiple times that she would love baseball to be fully coed, but also recognized these same issues with opportunities for female players, so the idea of girls-only baseball is something that allows girls to excel in baseball without being coerced into switching to softball like many people tried with Martha.

By expanding the game across gender lines, baseball would not be wasting its time and energy because plenty of those girls would be capable of playing at the next level. This is not to say that the genders of professional players would suddenly be equal if boys and girls had equal opportunities at the youth and high school level to play baseball, but there would certainly be several girls every year who excelled enough to play at the next level. Granted, we may never see a female version of Mike Trout, but a female version of Fuld, Altuve, or even Tim Wakefield (a pitcher who had a Little League quality fastball but a legendary knuckleball) could truly make an impact at the MLB level.

PLAYING IN THE CLOSET

In some ways, the closet has been a more isolated place for ballplayers than being Black or even female. Homophobia is a pandemic across nearly every sport, but within the world of baseball it has been notably difficult for any gay players to actually come out. The Kinsey Institute estimated that 10% of the population was gay and Major League Baseball has about 1000 players, so this would imply that there are roughly 100 players in the Majors who are gay. This is an oversimplification, however, because professional athletes are *not* representative of the population as a whole due to the many ways they are weeded out (literally one of the major points of this book), but if you look at Little League and similar levels, you will find that those ratios will be closer of the number of kids who grow up to eventually come out one day. The question is, do these kids all quit between Little League and pro ball, or do they simply hide their true selves from the public?

So far, it appears that Major League Baseball is not

accepting of gay players because there has yet to be an active major leaguer who was out to the public. There were some players who have come out privately to some teammates or who came out after retirement, but the fact that over 18,000 players have appeared in a Major League game and not one did so while openly gay should say a lot about how homosexuality is accepted in Major League clubhouses. Any player who has spent time in a men's locker room for any sport can attest to the fact that homophobia is one form of bigotry that is still generally considered socially acceptable. This isn't to say that it's okay to be homophobic in a locker room, but rather it means that a closeted player is likely to hear open homophobia expressed by their teammates on a very regular basis.

Some baseball players have been able to express themselves privately, but at the elite professional ranks it has been extremely rare and nobody has come out to the public while actively playing. The most prominent player to have ever come out of the closet would probably be Glenn Burke. Burke was not an elite player, but he was a guy who was good enough to play in 225 Major League games. Burke was out and openly gay to his teammates and the Dodgers organization, and that did not sit well with them. At one point, Al Campanis, a member of the Dodgers' front office, even offered to pay for his honeymoon if he got married to a woman. Eventually he was traded away when, according to teammates, the Dodgers' management decided they did not want a gay man in the clubhouse[lxxviii]. Burke has a place in sports history, too, because he was known to have given the first ever "high five". So, not only was he a trailblazer as a gay man in Major League Baseball, but he also started a trend that many people do not even realize has only been around since 1977.

Figure 7 (the first high five)

Although Burke definitely blazed a trail, he did not do so publicly. He existed in the shadows and fought to keep his life as normal as possible while having to hide a major piece of who he was from the public. After he was traded to Oakland, Burke started regularly for the Athletics in 1978, but he pinched a nerve in his neck and missed the majority of the 1979 season. In 1980 he returned to Oakland, with Billy Martin as the new manager. Martin was known for being a wild personality who rubbed a lot of people the wrong way. He was a brilliant manager who would often wear out his welcome in just a few years because of his personality. He did not welcome Burke with open arms. In the 2010 documentary "Out: The Glenn Burke Story," Athletics teammate Claudell Washington recalled how Martin introduce the new teammates that year: "Then he got to Glenn and said, 'Oh, by the way, this is Glenn Burke and he's a faggot.'"

His teammates were not comfortable around him, notably avoiding the showers when he was around and being sure to appear at a distance from him to not arouse suspicion. As A's outfielder Mitchell Page told *Inside Sports* in 1982: "I liked Glenn, but if I'd seen him walking around making it obvious, I wouldn't have had anything to do with him. I don't want to be labeled and have my career damaged...you make sure you point out that I'm not gay, okay?" Eventually the isolation he felt, in addition to a knee injury and his demotion to the minors, drove Burke to leave baseball altogether. Just two years later he came out to the public, the first former Major League player to do so in baseball history. "I had finally gotten to the point," he told *Inside Sports*, "where it was more important to be myself than a baseball player."

He revived his love for baseball by playing in gay leagues and starring in the Gay Olympics, but he struggled a lot after his Major League career ended, and he died of AIDS in the 1990s. When Burke published his memoir in 1995, he often stated how he had hoped his coming out would have had a bigger impact. In reality, the impact of him coming out was minimal in the grand scheme of things but he still was able to have an influence on many. "I think everyone just pretended not to hear me. It just wasn't a story they were ready to hear," he told People Magazine that year. Burke's struggle was significant, because gay players not only have to hide who they are from the public, but they also need to create a fake persona for their teammates who are generally macho and homophobic.

Times are certainly changing when it comes to the acceptance of gay players, but the biggest challenge with acceptance in sports is that locker rooms are already toxic environments to begin with. Athletes say stuff in the locker room that would never be said outside of one, and much of that stuff is sexual in nature. And much of what is said is stuff that most people would never admit to thinking, let alone expressing it out loud. The idea of "locker room talk" goes beyond the realm of sports, because this very term was used to describe the way that Donald Trump spoke about women to Billy Bush in the infamous Access Hollywood tapes released prior to the 2016 election. Many of the people I saw scoffing at the idea of "locker room talk" publicly on social media were teammates in the past that I had heard expressing these very same types of ideas. Notable is one high school teammate who is a very vocal feminist these days, but in high school he was the kind of guy who said a whole host of sexist and misogynist things on the bus rides to road games and in the locker room. In fact, I'm not beyond this, either. I would be lying if I said that I never once said something inappropriate within a sports setting. As a player, you can get caught up in the environment and become a person who is much different from who you are without that team. Many athletes change completely when they are part of a team. Some never change back. And some, like my former teammate, take such a hard turn in the other direction that they are unrecognizable from that version of themselves. Sports are more than just a game on the field. Many of us become completely engrossed within our sports and they become our way of life and our path through life.

Being gay in professional sports is still extremely rare,

but it is becoming more and more mainstream as the years go by. In 2018 a soccer player named Collin Martin came out as gay and a couple of years later he was involved in an incident during a game between his San Diego Loyal and the Phoenix Rising in the USL Championship, a second tier soccer league. A player on the Rising called Martin a slur relating to his status as a homosexual man and as a result, Martin's entire team walked off the field in protest. This dramatic move, partially spearheaded by Landon Donovan (one of the greatest American soccer players of all-time and the manager of the San Diego Loyal), showed the dramatic shift in the way that gay men are received in professional sports. Donovan was heard saying, "We have to get this out of our game...it's homophobia," before instructing his team to take a knee at the start of the second half before vacating the field and leaving the game altogether[lxxix]. Martin represents the courage to come out and Donovan represents the courage to support. Being gay in a men's sport is still extremely taboo. In my experience as an athlete, I always saw and heard more homophobia than any other troubling expression of opinion and it is still extremely prevalent in most sports.

Each sport is different, but it really appears that the feelings across all team sports are relatively equal. If you come out as gay to your teammates, you will face discrimination, bigotry, and ostracization. One caveat is that this mostly applies to men's sports, because women's sports are far more accepting of gay players, and in some cases the feelings of homophobia are actually reversed and the heterosexual players feel they are discriminated against[lxxx]. That's a really loaded statement and there is much debate about it, but it does show the ocean of difference between men's and women's sports. Jason Collins, a Stanford educated player with a heterosexual twin who also played in the NBA, came out of the closet in 2013 while still active in the NBA, but he was not a consequential player. The only reason Collins is remembered by anyone other than fans of his teams is because of the announcement he made on April 29, 2013. He played sparingly for another year in the NBA, playing a total of only 172 minutes and committing 30 fouls while scoring only 25 points the whole 2013–2014 season. He then left the NBA for good and it was again a league with zero players out of the closet. Eight years later, the league is still waiting for someone to follow Collins' path[lxxxi].

Another player who took a chance by coming out was pitcher Sean Conroy. As recounted in Ben Lindbergh and Sam Miller's book about running the 2015 Stompers, *The Only Rule Is It Has to Work*, Conroy came out to his parents when he was a teenager. They were immediately accepting but also worried. "I said, 'I think you should kinda keep it in your back pocket until you get through high school,'" Conroy's mother, Terry, told Lindbergh. "'It's just a better life, because I know what life was like when I was in high school.'" But Conroy had a better idea. Rather than stay in hiding, he came right out to his high school teammates. Later, he would do the same in college at Rensselaer Polytechnic Institute.[lxxxii] Conroy was honored in Cooperstown, commemorating his status as the first openly gay man to be active on a professional baseball roster, despite the fact that Conroy never really reached any upper tier of baseball. Conroy was a great college pitcher at the division 3 level, but his professional career stopped at the independent level. He did not break the MLB's barrier, just the professional baseball one. He retired in 2017, having only one significant incident of homophobia that he can recall. But the challenge was far less for Conroy than other players due to a number of things, not the least of which was simply having good teammates who were not caught up in hate.

Another pitcher around the same time as Conroy who came out as gay was Tyler Dunnington, but his story was very different from Conroy's. He was a pitcher for rookie and Class A teams affiliated with the Cardinals in 2014,303 Dunnington told *Outsports* he left pro ball because of homophobia. "I experienced both coaches and players make remarks on killing gay people during my time in baseball, and each comment felt like a knife to my heart," he said. "I was miserable in a sport that used to give me life." He quit in 2015 after one season and came out afterward[lxxxiii]. Dunnington had potential to eventually reach the Majors, but his experience in the minors and college, including once when a coach of his said, "We kill gay people in Wyoming," had a serious impact on him and took away his joy for the game he loved.

Being gay is not something that is identifiable on the surface (for the most part, there are obviously exceptions) like race is, so like with being Jewish, it is something that is up to the player to reveal to his teammates. But unlike being Jewish, being gay still comes with a significant stigma in athletic circles. Players have fears of showering with gay teammates, whereas they don't care about showering with a Jewish teammate. Players worry about being alone with a gay teammate, but they don't worry about being alone with a Jewish teammate. So, when a gay man happens to excel at baseball, he is far less likely to reveal the fact that he is gay because of that potential ostracization and isolation that can come from being different.

If the player chooses to keep his faith or sexual orientation private, he is likely to face a situation where his teammates are saying something offensive and he must decide whether to go along with it, speak out against it, or do what most athletes do and simply remain silent.

One player who was silent during his career but who has become one of the loudest voices in retirement is Billy Bean. Bean was a star athlete his whole life and could have easily played professional in any sport he put his mind to, but Bean was a baseball player to the core. As a kid he grew up in a place where being an MLB player was the goal for everyone his age. Everyone played Little League at his school and Billy was always one of the best. He was not just a baseball player, though, because Billy also played Pop Warner football and loved it. "Football was more exciting to me, and I could see why people today may be more interested in football over baseball[lxxxiv]". Bean maintained that love for football, but baseball began to take him to places that many of his peers could not go. Baseball was going to be his life's purpose. But Bean had a secret and it ate away at him on the inside.

Billy Bean is gay, but during his MLB career he was married to a woman. It wasn't until he was in his late 20s when he finally began to live more and more as a gay man. He did not come out of the closet publicly while he was playing, but he began to grow more comfortable living as his true self in private. However, he was still in a world where people like him were the butt of jokes and the target of hate, so he kept his true self secret from his teammates. "The only opinions that mattered to me were those of my peers", Bean said. "The only dialogue you would hear in the locker room in my days was sexism and homophobia and it was even celebrated. You could get away with whatever in those days before social media and smartphones, so you could keep secrets. You can't hide your race or gender very easily, but you can hide your sexuality." So that is exactly what Bean did. He hid.

"When you're gay in a straight household, it is frightening, because every image you see and everything you hear makes you think you're not right. I didn't live with my biological father, so I had a lot of that 'who am I? Where do I come from?' in me. They were perpetuating homophobia at my table because they didn't know there was a gay person in their house, especially because I did not fit the stereotype." This experience for Bean was deeply personal, but not unique. Countless others experience this same feeling at home, the feeling of being loved and accepted for who they think you are, but not for who you truly are. Bean was lucky because he was able to blend in as a typical jock and not face scrutiny. "I was never outwardly discriminated against because I was never accused of being gay. I was very careful to maintain my image. I did not present that way, people saw me as just another straight ballplayer. The internal dialogue was the biggest challenge. I am a sensitive person and I wanted to be accepted among my peers." Bean remained in the closet his entire MLB career, but he eventually became just the second former MLB player to come out.

"You can't hide your race or gender, but you can hide your sexuality. I didn't hear about positive gay role models, especially male ones. All I wanted to be was a baseball player. I lived in fear that my parents would find out. I wasn't being myself, I was not acting out on my feelings because I was afraid." Bean spoke candidly about his experience hiding in the closet. He struggled a lot with his fears of being rejected or ostracized by people he cared about, and he was hiding in the closet during a time period when the gay community was facing the AIDS epidemic head on. "The closet in the 80s and 90s when people were dying of AIDS was a scary place. I thought I may be HIV positive, and I felt guilt about my partner's death from HIV." Bean still holds the pain from decades ago because of his inability to fight it at the time.

"I was hiding my partner from my own family while I was playing near my family. When I found my partner, Sam, I started playing baseball at a level I never played before. But when he got sick, it beat me up. I was fearful of being told I was HIV positive because I had been exposed." Bean speaks about his past with such perspective that it almost seems as if he is a biographer narrating the story of his life. "But I did not want to do anything because I was so worried about being found out. I was starting to fit in and play a lot and then it just changed so fast. All of the stereotypes I had grown up with were the homophobia I was dealing with and I carried it on my back. Baseball was not cruel to me, baseball just thought I was fumbling my opportunity. When my partner died, I did not even go to his funeral." The pain of missing the funeral of his partner clearly sticks with him to this day. "I felt like I was turning the corner when Sam died, but then all those negative thoughts came flooding back. My family did not make me feel that way and my teammates did not do anything to hurt me or make me feel bad. It was mainly the internal struggle that caused the issues for me."

The internal struggle of playing in the closet is significant. The fear of being found out takes a serious toll on any person hiding a secret, and it is especially significant when that person is in the public eye. The secret has a weight that can derail even the most talented people from their path. Billy Bean was not the first gay MLB player and he was certainly not the last one. The simple fact that there is not even one player in the MLB in 2021 that is publicly out of the closet is a sign that there is much work to be done. Either all the gay kids felt so ostracized that they all left the sport before making it to the highest levels, or (more realistically) the gay players who have made it big feel so worried about potential discrimination or other issues that they hide who they truly are from the public. Public opinion on gay men in sports is still an issue that is evolving, but 2021 is certainly more welcoming to the idea than 1981 was.

However, public opinion on homosexuality still remains divided. As a teacher, I have experienced the post-millennial generation and their evolving attitudes about sexuality and gender. Kids today are far more open than thirty years ago and it shows in language. Terms like "Latinx" and "Womxn" exist now because people wish to show their support for marginalized communities and to provide perspective on the wider spectrum of gender and sexuality than many people tend to think about. That said, coastal cities are far more likely to be "evolved" on this issue. Kids at a rural school in Mississippi are far less likely to have positive feelings towards homosexuality than kids in Massachusetts. One study showed that adults in Mississippi are 54% likely to discourage homosexuality compared to just 12% in Massachusetts. The same study showed that adults in Massachusetts are 82% likely to accept homosexuality while only 40% of Mississippi residents are[lxxxv]. This disparity means the social movements we see on social media generally do not carry the same kind of weight in the Deep South as they do in New England. Unfortunately, many people within these movements are blinded by their allegiance to the movement and do not truly get that they are years ahead of where most of the country is. So while teachers find it perfectly normal to put their pronouns after their name on their email signature, farmers in Mississippi probably do not even know why it is even necessary to do so.

These important distinctions must be made if we are going to understand how progress is to be made. There are certainly several gay men playing professional baseball today, but the real question is how do we make them feel comfortable enough to come out so the next generation does not have to worry about it? Jackie Robinson had to answer tons of questions about being Black, whereas Barry Bonds did not. So, while the first generation of gay players will face bigotry, hate, discrimination, and an uphill battle to succeed in the MLB, the next generation will be empowered by their struggle. It cannot just be the random players, either—there have to be prominent players who come out. A Jason Collins does not have the same impact that a Jackie Robinson has. If a borderline player comes out of the closet and struggles slightly, the franchise can quietly send them down and forget about them. But if an all-star or elite pitcher comes out, it will be very hard for that player to quietly disappear from the league like Jason Collins did. While Collins may have inspired the next player to come out, he did not stick around long enough to truly impact the game by changing the attitudes of teammates and opponents about what it means to be gay.

SO, WHAT NEXT?

In this book we have explored many different problems relating to discrimination in sports, but few solutions have been offered. The main issue with these problems is that they are very difficult to solve due to the fact that they happen at the micro-level. They require changing the overall attitudes of millions of people and that is usually a generational thing. Baseball is a sport that is highly based in the community, and as a result, it has to be the communities that change. Little League in San Francisco is obviously different from Little League in South Central LA, and those are an ocean apart from the leagues in rich suburban neighborhoods in the South. A kid growing up gay and Black in San Francisco would likely feel more accepted than that same kid would feel in other places of the country. Some places will be quicker to change than others and some places will fight progress.

As we saw in the experiences of players like Terry

Whitfield and Wilmer Aaron, racism did not just end when the Civil Rights act was passed. Segregation may have been illegal, but it was not over. Black players had to fight to find a decent place to stay, while their White teammates were welcomed with open arms. Black players had to deal with coaches seeing them as "wrong for their position," when their White teammates were able to excel in the position of their choice. As baseball has shifted more and more towards the highly specialized niche sport it is today, many Black players left the sport because it required giving up on other sports where they felt more welcomed and saw far more people like them at the professional ranks.

We often discount the value of simply seeing someone who represents a traditionally oppressed or marginalized group achieving great success, but the value of breaking a glass ceiling cannot be overstated. My teenage niece is growing up in a world where she can not only strive to be an Olympic athlete (modern pentathlon, of all things), but also where she can set a goal of becoming a Supreme Court Justice like her hero, Justice Sonia

Sotomayor. These are career goals that her great grandmother could not have had in her time, regardless of how progressive and strong my grandmother was. My son was born after the election of the first female Vice President and was born into a world where people like him, those with multi-ethnic backgrounds, have now been President and Vice President. But these markers do not change the fact that while in big cities we see a lot of positive movement on social justice, in small towns across America we are seeing the opposite occur. Social media has radicalized countless people and given rise to new generations of bigoted individuals raised on a whole new flavor of bigotry. Facts and experiences matter less than buzzwords and memes and many people live in an insular world where reality does not penetrate. So, while we are seeing huge numbers of people opening up to new ideas, some of those ideas are contrary to social justice.

Progress is never a one-way street; it can often take twists and turns that were never expected or intended. But progress does not happen by accident, and it does not come to those who simply wait for it. People have to fight for it. If one person can change the opinion of just two people, it can eventually turn into a tsunami, where a once popular opinion is rendered obsolete. This is easier said than done, though, because shifting popular opinions is extremely difficult and often takes generations to be fully realized. As we continue to strive for a society where people feel accepted for who they are, one of the main goals has to be within the messaging. We live in a world where we have unlimited access to information, but the information can be tainted through messaging. Much of today's divided political climate is exacerbated by messaging and misleading headlines.

Oftentimes the same exact story is copied word-for-word on an online article but the headline is wildly different. One article may say "man injured in car accident" while the other article may say "White man injured in accident caused by illegal immigrant". Both are reporting on the same incident, but one version of the article is neutral and the other is dripping with a specific political opinion. This example is fictional, but the practice of creating clickbait headlines is growing exponentially as the media continues to realize the impact of a headline on clicks. Writing headlines to draw clicks is nothing new, but it has become more and more mainstream for large media corporations to do. Going to CNN or Fox News will lead you to dozens of articles with headlines that simply do not paint the whole picture, but rather provide you with a teaser of what is included in the article. Many articles leave out key information in a headline and go with the "people react to so-and-so's statement" type of headline that says nothing but still entices a reader to click. The more vague and partisan the headline, the more likely it is to get clicks.

The pay-per-click nature of news these days means that articles talking about controversial topics will always be read more than those talking about more basic situations, and bad news always travels much faster than good news. So, if a Black player is arrested for domestic violence, that'll be plastered all over every news station, but if a Black player visits kids in the hospital and hands out food to the homeless, that player is unlikely to get much press for it at all. This does impact all people, but the impact is far more significant for people of color and for women than it is for White men. Even the way people are physically perceived varies by race. Black men are considered to be bigger and stronger than White men and it gets even more nefarious than that as we consider the studies done.

One study concluded that not only do people think Black men are bigger and stronger than White men, but that they are also more dangerous. A study was done in which about 1000 participants were shown pictures of Black and White men and then asked about their size and potential to be a threat. In the study, participants judged the Black men to be larger, stronger, and more muscular than the White men, even though they were actually the same size. Additionally, they believed that the Black men were more capable of causing harm in a hypothetical altercation and, troublingly, that police would be more justified in using force to subdue them, even if the men were unarmed[lxxxvi]. While this book has mostly been about baseball, the sport is merely a lens through which we can see our problems with race, gender, sexual orientation, and personal identity truly reveal themselves. As with any problem, the roots run much deeper than how it appears on the surface and the solution is neither easy nor simple.

For every person who has their mind changed or who goes out and tries to impact the world, there are dozens of others who continue on with the status quo or who actively fight against progress. For every Curt Flood willing to put his career on the line, there is a Solly Hemus working to keep him from his success. Flood's triumph came at great personal cost and Wilmer Aaron never even got to achieve his goal. Billy Bean hid in the shadows. Justine Siegal faced headwinds at every turn. These great athletes all took different paths and had wildly different levels of success along the way. The long-term impact of each cannot be measured either, because Wilmer's impact on

Dominic Smith and all the other kids he has coached over the years cannot be quantified. The impact of Bean's work in the administrative offices of MLB is impossible to truly measure. The breadth of Terry Whitfield's impact on the Bay Area baseball community is immeasurable. Who knows how many kids Vida Blue will impact through his community work? Simply put, the attempt is what truly matters.

There is no scorecard for impact. Nobody is keeping track and you don't earn points for it. The impact is not always felt immediately and it is not always obvious. I am a teacher and sometimes I have students who drive me absolutely bonkers. They disrupt class, they talk back, they show obvious disrespect, and it seems as if I am having no impact on them whatsoever. Then one day, I'll get a message out of the blue. One such message came to me after my father died and I posted about it on social media. The note read: "Just wanted to let you know you're a really good dude and I appreciate all you did for me when I was at DPAC. You were one of the only people who actually believed in me so thank you and keep your head high. Despite the hard time I gave you and all the shit I talked I really respect you at the end of the day and I know out of everyone you and a select few actually cared about my future." I honestly did not realize that I had that kind of impact on the kid. I make sure to tell my old coaches that I use their drills or training techniques with my players, but I guarantee that I am not the only man who tells pitchers "balance, shoulder to the target, follow through" and who tells them to read "Golf is Not a Game of Perfect" because Fred Breining taught me that way.

In the end, we have to understand that being progressive means that you are leading from the front, not pushing from the back. You cannot worry about what people say and do if you truly want to make a real impact. You may never see your impact directly, but if you fight to make it happen you will have a chance at success. Having an impact is not about the rewards or the adulation. Vida Blue never made the Hall of Fame, and Curt Flood still sits on the outside of Cooperstown, too. But those two men have impacted generations with their work on and off the field. I can only hope to have the same kind of impact.

ACKNOWLEDGEMENTS

Special thanks to the following people

Billy Bean

Vida Blue

Curt Flood Jr.

John Murdzek

Joanne Pasternack

Martha Rodriguez

Justine Siegal

Terry Whitfield

And a very special thanks to Wilmer Aaron, without whom I would have never started on this journey and who provided me with the inspiration to share his story with the world.

REFERENCES

[i] Schwarz, Alan; Thorn, John (2004). "From Babe to Mel – The Top 100 People in Baseball History". *Hank Aaron. Total Baseball: The Ultimate Baseball Encyclopedia*. Wilmington, Delaware: Sport Media Publishing Inc. p. 819

[ii] Spencer, Lauren (2002). *Hank Aaron*. Baseball Hall of Famers. New York: Rosen Central. p. 27

[iii] Schwartz, Larry (1999). "Hammerin' back at racism". ESPN Classic. Archived from the original on November 18, 2010.

[iv] Stanton, Tom (2005). *Hank Aaron and the Home Run That Changed America*. New York: Perennial Currents. P. 179

[v] https://www.vice.com/en/article/eze4v4/do-premier-league-managers-pigeonhole-Black-players

[vi] http://richmondfreepress.com/news/2020/jun/04/where-are-african-american-catchers-mlb/

[vii] https://www.usatoday.com/story/sports/columnist/bob-nightengale/2016/04/14/mlb-jackie-robinson-african-american-players-pitchers/83052454/

[viii] Thorpe, Dave "Wilmer Aaron resigns as Serra High baseball coach". Daily Breeze. November 10, 2015

[ix] https://twitter.com/TheRealSmith2_/status/1272225800721489926?s=20

[x] https://morningconsult.com/2020/09/10/sports-fan-base-demographic-data/

[xi] Plaschke, Bill (2013). "Baseball is diamond in the rough to Black players at Gardena Serra". Los Angeles Times. May 14, 2013.

[xii] http://www.usaschoolinfo.com/school/junipero-serra-high-school-san-mateo-california.104485/

[xiii] "Gardena (city) QuickFacts". United States Census Bureau. Archived from the original on March 17, 2015. Retrieved March 10, 2015.

[xiv] "2007-2011 American Community Survey 5-Year Estimates". *United States Census Bureau*. 2011. Archived from the original on February 12, 2020. Retrieved April 8, 2020.

[xv] Aaron, Wilmer - Private Correspondence

[xvi] http://www.espn.com/espn/eticket/story?page=bostock

[xvii] https://miscbaseball.wordpress.com/2008/12/17/the-murder-of-lyman-bostock-in-1978/

[xviii] Ibid.,

[xix] http://www.espn.com/espn/eticket/story?page=bostock

[xx] https://sabr.org/sites/default/files/MLB-Demographics-Armour-Levitt-Figure1.png

[xxi] Aaron, Wilmer - Private Correspondence

[xxii] https://sabr.org/research/article/baseball-demographics-1947-2012/

[xxiii] Personal conversation with Curt Flood, Jr.

[xxiv] https://scholarship.law.nd.edu/cgi/viewcontent.cgi?article=1000&context=baseball_salaries

[xxv] https://www.espn.com/mlb/story/_/id/31270164/average-mlb-salary-417-million-48-2019

[xxvi] https://www.spotrac.com/mlb/rankings/earnings/all-time/

[xxvii] https://www.sandiegouniontribune.com/sports/padres/story/2021-03-31/padres-2021-opening-day-payroll

[xxviii] Correspondence with Curt Flood Jr.

[xxix] https://www.latimes.com/archives/la-xpm-1993-01-05-me-833-story.html

[xxx] https://sabr.org/bioproj/person/fleet-walker/

[xxxi] https://sabr.org/gamesproj/game/may-2-1887-the-first-african-american-battery/

[xxxii] Rosenberg. *Cap Anson 4.*, pp. 427-428.

[xxxiii] https://dazzyvancechronicles.wordpress.com/2015/03/11/manager-mcgraw-wanted-to-do-the-right-thing/

[xxxiv] https://www.complex.com/sports/2017/05/ugly-history-boston-being-most-racist-sports-city-america

[xxxv] Sullivan, N. (1998). Baseball and Race: The Limits of Competition. *The Journal of Negro History, 83*(3), 168-177.

[xxxvi] https://www.si.com/mlb/2020/06/10/boston-red-sox-confirm-torii-hunter-racist-slurs-fenway-park

[xxxvii] https://www.schooldigger.com/go/CA/district/34320/search.aspx

[xxxviii] https://www.sandiegouniontribune.com/sports/sd-sp-san-diego-inner-city-baseball-struggles-20170517-story.html

[xxxix] Ibid.,

[xl] https://www.sandiegounified.org/demographic_data

[xli] http://www.thebaseballcube.com/hs/byRegion.asp?R=CA

[xlii] https://vimeo.com/355614285

[xliii] https://usctrojans.com/sports/baseball/roster/jaden-agassi/11764

[xliv] KLEIN, GARY (May 22, 1990). "Program Brings Baseball Back to inner-city - Los Angeles Times"

[xlv] Personal conversation with Terry Whitfield, September 12, 2020

[xlvi] https://www.baltimoresun.com/news/bs-xpm-1995-06-05-1995156073-story.html

[xlvii] https://www.baseball-reference.com/teams/SFG/leaders_bat_50.shtml

[xlviii] Personal conversation with Terry Whitfield, September 12, 2020

[xlix] Personal conversation with Vida Blue, August 30, 2020

[l] https://www.thehawkeye.com/sports/20200425/blue-recalls-burlington-beginning

[li] https://news.wttw.com/2020/06/08/having-talk-how-families-prepare-Black-children-police-interactions

[lii] https://theundefeated.com/features/the-only-mlb-all-star-game-that-featured-two-african-american-starting-pitchers/

[liii] Ibid.,

[liv] https://sabr.org/bioproj/person/vida-blue/

[lv] Ibid.,

[lvi]e4r4c https://frntofficesport.com/little-league-participation/

[lvii] https://www.usatoday.com/story/sports/mlb/2019/08/23/put-me-in-coach-youth-baseball-participation-on-the-rise/40002827/

[lviii] https://d1baseballoffer.com/2018/03/11/youth-travel-baseball-how-much-does-it-really-cost-parents/

[lix] https://www.cdc.gov/nchs/data/nhsr/nhsr071.pdf

[lx] https://news.berkeley.edu/2020/03/04/why-are-american-public-schools-still-segregated/

[lxi] These results are all anecdotal from my own experience with Crawford High School and DPAC HS

[lxii] https://bleacherreport.com/articles/1982932-in-search-of-the-hardest-thing-to-do-in-baseball

[lxiii] https://www.espn.com/espn/story/_/id/27308702/study-average-child-quits-sports-age-11

[lxiv] https://remezcla.com/features/sports/the-secret-history-of-how-mexico-pushed-baseball-toward-racial-integration/

[lxv] Ibid.,

[lxvi] Ibid.,

[lxvii] https://www.dailychela.com/black-players-once-dominated-mexican-baseball/

[lxviii] Personal conversation with Martha Rodriguez, April 2021

[lxix] Personal Interview with Justine Siegal January 14, 2021

[lxx] https://spreadsheetsolving.com/little-league/

[lxxi] Perrotto, John (July 11, 2016). "Novelty no more: Astros' Jose Altuve in the conversation as one of baseball's best". *USA Today.*

[lxxii] Justice, Richard (April 29, 2018). "Altuve 'went against all the odds' to reach Majors: Pedrique knew then-16-year-old Venezuelan had what it takes". *MLB.com.*

[lxxiii] https://ukathletics.com/news/2020/5/4/softball-bailey-vick-to-forgo-extra-year-will-graduate-and-start-finance-career.aspx

[lxxiv] https://jmusports.com/sports/softball/roster/kate-gordon/16466

[lxxv] https://nmstatesports.com/sports/baseball/roster/nick-gonzales/6179

[lxxvi] https://www.baseball-reference.com/register/player.fcgi?id=gonzal004nic

[lxxvii] https://bleacherreport.com/articles/1128801-dee-gordon-is-embarrassing-the-experts-that-said-he-was-too-small-to-excel

[lxxviii] https://www.washingtonpost.com/news/morning-mix/wp/2015/08/17/the-trials-of-baseballs-first-openly-gay-player-glenn-burke-four-decades-ago/

[lxxix] https://sports.yahoo.com/san-diego-loyal-phoenix-uprising-landon-donovan-collin-martin-usl-050140214.html

[lxxx] https://www.courant.com/sports/basketball/hc-wiggins-wnba-0222-20170221-story.html

[lxxxi] https://sports.yahoo.com/there-is-that-fear-jason-collins-first-openly-gay-nba-player-on-why-there-hasnt-been-a-second-170207408.html

[lxxxii] https://bleacherreport.com/articles/2652165-1-year-later-pro-baseballs-1st-openly-gay-player-still-leads-by-example

[lxxxiii] https://weeeeww.advocate.com/sports/2018/2/02/17-baseball-heroes-who-came-out-gay

[lxxxiv] Personal interview with Billy Bean January 7, 2021

[lxxxv] https://www.pewforum.org/religious-landscape-study/compare/views-about-homosexuality/by/state/

[lxxxvi] https://www.cnn.com/2017/03/13/health/Black-men-larger-study-trnd/index.html

Made in the USA
Monee, IL
13 February 2023

27717632R00125